WEALTHY
AND WISE

WEALTHY AND WISE

A PRACTICAL GUIDE TO HELP PHYSICIANS PROTECT THEIR ASSETS, MAXIMIZE THEIR ESTATES, AND RETIRE HAPPY

Michael Jankowski

ISBN: 1539589412
ISBN 13: 9781539589419

Like my own family, your family needs wealth protection planning.

INTRODUCTION

Michael Jankowski

From a very young age, I grew up with a passion for investing. My father began his career as a welder for Caterpillar Tractor Company and, over a twenty-five-year career, worked his way into upper management. He wholeheartedly believed in Caterpillar's world-class products and saved by purchasing Caterpillar stock through the company's payroll deduction. Since my dad had most of his retirement money in Caterpillar stock, he followed their price closely. He taught me how to read and follow Caterpillar's stock price at the age of thirteen. The entire process of investing in the stock market amazed me, even at that young age.

My mom was a stay-at-home mother to my three siblings and me. We lived a modest yet comfortable life. My father instilled a strong work ethic as far back as I can remember and expected my siblings and me to acquire jobs at a young age. To this day, I carry on that same work ethic that I so respected seeing in my dad as a young child. My father maintained, if we didn't see ourselves at the same job for at least five years, it wasn't the career path for us. That was a sentiment I carried forward.

Curious to learn more about how the stock markets worked, I began to immerse myself in the complex world of finance and investments. At my young age, I found everything I read to be complex and confusing. I would go to the local library and scan the daily *Wall Street Journal*, finding myself reading an article several times to grasp only a small portion of the technical concepts the author was describing. I then came across a book, *One Up on Wall Street* by Peter Lynch, who managed the Fidelity Magellan Fund and was best known for his straightforward back-to-the-basics style of investing. He managed to outperform the S&P 500 index by a wide margin over his tenure while taking on less risk.

In his book, he described his investment philosophy, ideas, and concepts in a manner that the average non-investor could comprehend. Furthermore, he made it enjoyable for the reader. His book inspired me to continue to pursue my quest for understanding the world of finance and investments.

In my first year of college, my father was killed in an automobile accident at the age of forty-five. I immediately recognized the devastating repercussions in failing to have a proper financial and estate plan in place. Of course this was a tragic and unexpected event, yet as much as my father planned and saved for the future, a financial and estate plan apparently took a backseat in his planning process. This lapse in judgement took a devastating toll on my mom and all of us.

Unfortunately Caterpillar stock was trading at a fifty-two-week low due to the economy being in a recession. My father had very little life insurance; nor did he have a will or trust. Since my mother was not named as a joint owner on most of the Caterpillar stock, she had to hire an attorney to go through the probate process in order to have the stock transferred into her name. We were obviously unprepared for his untimely death. I became propelled to follow my passion for investments and finance but apply my knowledge in a way that could help other families prepare for unintended financial consequences.

Fast-forward thirty years. I run my own wealth advisory firm, Wealth Planning Network, and have given hundreds of educational seminars sharing my knowledge and passion for proper financial and estate planning and tax reduction that people need to enable them to retire financially secure while protecting their heirs from those unintended financial consequences. As you read the book, remember that I am not just the author but a family member whose life was directly impacted by the negative experiences of the lack of wealth protection planning.

I dedicate this book to all my clients. I am truly blessed by the client relationships I have built over my twenty-five-year career. I am grateful to all my clients and their families who have entrusted me over the years to guide them through their own wealth protection planning. Thank you!

PART I

THE MARKETS AND YOUR RETIREMENT

Wealth is nothing more or less than a tool to do things with. It is like the fuel that runs the furnace or the belt that runs the wheel—only a means to an end.
HENRY FORD

CHAPTER 1

BRACING FOR IMPACT IN AN UNPREDICTABLE WORLD

L ike most Americans, I watched in horror as the twin towers of the World Trade Center crumbled to the ground on September 11, 2001. When the first plane hit the North Tower, I thought it was just an accident. I think most people thought that perhaps some inexperienced pilot had lost control of a small plane. I dimly remembered hearing about a World War II bomber, lost in the fog over Manhattan, crashing into the Empire State Building. Maybe something like that had happened again.

Then the second jetliner hit the South Tower, and the slow realization washed over me that our nation was under attack. I don't think the enormity of what had happened registered on any of us at first. We were glued to our televisions that day, but none of us quite knew how to wrap our minds around the tragedy. The networks kept airing the events of the day over and over. Planes crashing, the buildings falling, and people running for their lives. The images made us heartsick, but we were unable to turn away. It was as if continually revisiting the shock and pain was a way to cope with it and heal from it.

That tragedy showed Americans just how quickly our world can change. One minute everything can be rolling right along, going according to plan, and the next minute the roof can cave in. Fortunately, it is within the American framework to rebound. It seems to be part of our national DNA to survive our tragedies, meet our challenges head-on, learn from hard times, and emerge better and stronger for the experience.

But what happened on 9/11 was etched on our collective consciousness like a laser. We still see the posters and signs bearing the words "Never Forget," a slogan that urges remembrance for that national tragedy. For those of us who watched those events unfold, I don't think forgetting is an option.

Those of us who carefully observe the nation's economy will likely never forget what happened to the stock market after 9/11. The New York Stock Exchange (NYSE), only a few blocks from Ground Zero, did not open on the day of the attacks. The Wall Street barons, to prevent a stock market meltdown, chose to suspend trading for the rest of the week. They announced that trading would not resume until Monday, September 17, the longest closure of the market since the Great Depression forced a cessation of trading in 1933.

When the market did reopen, the Dow Jones Industrial Average (DJIA) stock market index fell 684 points, or 7.1 percent, to 8920, its biggest-ever one-day point decline in history at that point. The market did recover somewhat from the panic selling, but then starting in March 2002, it lapsed into a steady decline with dramatic dips in July and September. Eventually the stock market bumped bottoms last reached in 1997 and 1998, a period now referred to as the recession of 2002–2003.

The mood of the investing public was nervous. There had been upswings and downturns in the past, but there was an uneasy feeling throughout the nation that this kind of volatility was out of the ordinary. Those feelings were justified. What has been described as "the lost decade" for American investors had begun.

In retrospect, the terrorist acts of 9/11 might have triggered a market crash, but it did not cause the subsequent recession. When the attack occurred, the US economy was already in a transition from an unsustainable rate of growth to what was hoped to be a more sustainable one. There had been rapid growth in the glory days of the 1990s. If you owned stocks in that decade, you remember how you could do no wrong. If you tossed a dart at the financial page, wherever the point landed, you could buy the stock and were sure to be a winner.

But then the dot-com bubble burst. Millions who were heavily invested in tech stocks lost fortunes. Industrial production began to decline in June 2000. Unemployment rose.

The US economy was already in trouble before the events of 9/11 took place. Looking back, it is clear that while Osama bin Laden and his band of fanatic extremists were plotting terror for America, the nation's economy was contracting, and conditions were ripe for recession. As tragic as those events were, what happened on September 11, 2001, didn't cause the recession that followed. It would have occurred anyway.

Corporate Disasters

Just as natural disasters leave ruined lives and devastation in their wake, corporate disasters can wreak financial havoc on investors' lives. Like those sinkholes you read about in Florida that occasionally open up and swallow homes and cars, the financial ground you are standing on could appear firm one moment and crumble beneath your feet the next.

Take the Enron debacle, for example. The Houston-based energy giant, the darling of Wall Street in the 1990s, was once valued at $90 billion and was the seventh-largest company in America. Corporate leaders weren't happy just being the leader in the energy sector. They started to diversify into other areas, the Internet and, of all things, weather futures.

When their ventures started to turn sour, their accountants became creative and painted a rosy financial picture of Enron just to keep the share prices high. Hiding debt and inflating profits finally caused the house of cards to collapse, and Enron declared bankruptcy in 2001.

The tragedy was how many people were hurt. I'm not just talking about the jobs that were lost. Thousands of Enron employees had sunk their life savings into Enron stock, and their portfolios were suddenly worthless. When you hear the name Enron now, your mental picture is of greedy executives shredding documents and the tattered financial lives of those who had their trust betrayed.

On the heels of the Enron disaster came the bankruptcy in 2002 of telecommunications giant, WorldCom, which at one time boasted $107 billion in assets. It made international news as the largest bankruptcy filing in American history to that point. Like Enron, WorldCom was also fond of "creative accounting," posting questionable earnings to fool Wall Street after it began losing money to changing technology

> *"Those who cannot learn from history are doomed to repeat it."* ~
> **George Santayana**

and competition. Company accountants inflated WorldCom assets by some $12 billion. Investors lost millions, and corporate executives responsible for the fraud were arrested, tried, and sent to prison.

The fall of Enron and then WorldCom was a nasty business that shook the confidence of American investors to the core and left them wondering if dishonesty and greed were par for the course among large national corporations.

The 2008 Market Crash

After 2003, Wall Street was quick to brush off the issues of years past, and the mood of American investors was almost euphoric. The memory of the 2000 Wall Street collapse had faded, and the dot-com bust was now considered just a bump in the road. Many felt as if the glory days of the 1990s were back again and the stock market would continue soaring heavenward as it had before. Dark clouds were gathering on the horizon, but few noticed them or gave them much thought.

[1]As 2007 began, the DJIA cruised past 12,400 and was galloping along while some warned of a housing bubble. But the sound of hammers putting up houses and condos and the roar of the money waterfall that was funding it drowned out all those warnings. Mortgage lenders were passing out home loans to anyone they thought could make the payments. Construction companies were putting up houses on speculation, and home buyers were in a feeding frenzy to snap them up. The way the banks looked at it, property values would continue to increase.

---

1 (Tully, Shawn (2006-05-05). "Welcome to the Dead Zone". *Fortune.*)

There was no way they could lose. If someone defaulted on a loan, they repossessed a property that, in a few years, would be double what it was when it was constructed.

At the top of the food chain were the mega banks responsible for the money flow. These were the too-big-to-fail banks, many of which would be insolvent by the end of 2008. In August 2007, when the Federal Reserve began to notice a liquidity problem caused by the easy-money policies set by these lending institutions, the Fed began to take measures to shore them up by pumping money into the system. Some saw this as proof that the economy was on thin ice. Banks were taking on more risk, and the poison of subprime mortgage debt was slowly working its way into the mega banks. Banks were taking on more and more risk, and the poison of subprime mortgage debt was slowly working its way into the veins of financial institutions that were "too big to fail."

A May 2006 *Fortune* magazine report on the housing bubble said, "The great housing bubble has finally started to deflate ...In many once-sizzling markets around the country, accounts of dropping list prices have replaced tales of waiting lists for unbuilt condos and bidding wars over humdrum three-bedroom colonials."[1]

[2]The small dominos began falling in 2007 when property values fell precipitously, and millions of homeowners found themselves owing considerably more for their houses than the houses were worth. In 2008, we watched the big dominos fall, as one bank after another began cracking up. Lehman Brothers, the fourth-largest investment bank in America, filed for the largest bankruptcy in US history. The venerable old Bear Stearns, known for making good business decisions for more than eight decades, spiraled from healthy to near insolvency in just seventy-two hours. The meltdown included other big names like Merrill Lynch, AIG, Freddie Mac, Fannie Mae, and Morgan Stanley. If the American economy were a car, all the idiot lights would have been blinking red.

In eight consecutive trading days in October, the DJIA would lose 2,399.47 points, or 22.11 percent. The following recession would be the longest and deepest in history and would drive the unemployment

---

2   (Isidore, Chris (2011-06-09) "America's Lost Trillions" CNN Money.)

rate up to 10 percent by October 2009. According to CNN Money, the Great Recession of 2008 lasted three years and cost Americans $16.4 trillion.[2]

When I tell you the US national debt is near $20 trillion and rising (at the time of this writing), what mental picture do you see? Sadly, most people shrug their shoulders. It's just too much to comprehend. If you take a trip to New York City and journey up the steel concrete canyons to the intersection of West 44th Street and Avenue of the Americas, you will see something that has become somewhat of a landmark, the Durst National Debt Clock.

It's about the size of a small billboard and has two running totals in the style of a digital odometer. One is the national debt; the other is "your family's share." The clock was the brainchild of New York real estate developer Seymour Durst, who wanted to publicize the country's runaway debt in 1989 when it was a mere $3 trillion. Durst died in 1995 and did not live to see his clock chronicle the $10 trillion milestone of 2008. When the debt exceeded $10 trillion in 2008, his heirs, the keepers of the clock, had to add another digit just to keep up. They continue to maintain the clock.

If you'd like to see where we're at today, just visit www.usdebtclock. org, and you will see Durst's two original calculations and scores of others that are equally as disturbing. If you are like me, you can't stop looking at the numbers as they whiz like an automobile odometer out of control. It adds a kinetic feel to the statistics and makes you feel a bit vulnerable as a citizen of a wealthy country. There is no other way to put it. That is spending like a drunken sailor. Worse really. Even a drunken sailor stops spending once he is out of money.

America's national debt might seem abstract, like something far away from reality. But if left unchecked, those whizzing numbers will spell big trouble for the great middle class in the form of higher interest rates and a weaker economy.

Let me share an example with you. A young man inherited a little over $110,000, and he decided to open a pizza restaurant. He leased a building and burned through the inheritance, buying ovens, tables, and chairs. He had a superb credit rating at the time and began using his credit cards, just knowing that future profits would quickly pay off the credit card debt. He splashed the newspapers with advertising, printed up and distributed flyers and coupons, and even hired a sidewalk clown for opening day. By now he was using his credit cards to pay bills. His rationalized that it took money to make money and debt was a precursor to wealth.

Sadly his restaurant did not go over very well in the community. He made delicious pizzas, but his place was too far off the road. As he learned, poor location is a killer in the restaurant business. After a few months of borrowing from one credit card to pay the minimum payment on another, he closed up shop and went back to his old job. The credit card debt was now over $100,000, and he couldn't earn enough to dig his way out. He had to declare personal bankruptcy, and he was forced to liquidate everything he owned.

He could have done things differently from the outset to protect his family and himself from the fallout of a business failure. That's true. But the point is, debt, even the debt of a country that can print its own money, will eventually be paid. Many people who watch the economic scene are worried about their government. When will politicians stop maxing out the nation's credit cards?

If you max out your credit cards, you can keep the spending spree going as long as you can come up with the money to make the minimum monthly payments. When you start to miss those, the creditors lose faith in you, and the collection phone calls start. Uncle Sam's creditors are spread throughout the globe.

At the time this book is being written, America relies on foreign investment to fund more than half of its debt. That's shocking to the conservative mind, but so far there is enough international appetite for American debt to keep the party going. But even the hint that the largest debtor nation in the world would not be able to pay up would send the world economy into chaos. Economically speaking, the United States is *sui generis* (in a class by itself).

It's too big to be compared to any other debtor nation, like Greece or Italy. It is so large that it redefines the word "solvency." The dollar is the king of world currency. No other country in the world has the luxury of borrowing so easily as America does. But make no mistake: debts weaken a country.

Questions to which there is no answer remain:

- At what point will US Treasury bonds cease to be attractive?
- Will the debt pressure produce higher interest rates, a lowering of the value of the dollar, or both?
- How much higher will taxes be raised to whittle down the debt?
- What form will that taxation take?
- What impact will it have on economic growth?
- How will it affect our standard of living and the core values of our nation?

Those are questions of national interest. On a more personal level, one may ask questions like,

- With so much uncertainty in the air, how should I invest?
- Should I continue to view market-based investing in the same light?
- How can I guarantee that I will not run out of money after I retire?
- Are there any guarantees?
- What strategies could I employ that would give me solid financial footing in retirement so I can sleep?

These and other questions will be addressed in subsequent chapters.

CHAPTER 2

LEARNING MARKET RISK THE HARD WAY

I n April 2007, John, age sixty-four and a half, woke up, yawned, and stretched before padding into the kitchen for his morning cup of coffee. It was a glorious spring morning. The sky was robin's egg blue, and the sun was already warming the day.

"Life is good," John thought to himself.

One of the reasons John was happy was that, after more than three decades on the job with the corporation he worked for, he was now only a few months away from retirement. He was looking forward to the big day when he said, "Good-bye, office. Hello, golf course."

John was feeling pretty good about things. He had been a good saver and investor. He had faithfully contributed to his company's 401(k) retirement plan and had ridden the roller coaster of the stock market through its ups and downs. Some years it was a nail-biter, but he held on for the recovery, which had always come. He had a little over $1.5 million in his retirement account, and that was not chump change!

"Won't it be nice," said his wife Jenny, "to take our time, knowing we don't have to come back home until we want to."

They also looked forward to spending time with their three grandchildren as well, a luxury that, until now, time had not afforded them.

Fast-forward to Monday, September 29, 2008. The day started with his usual routine, first the coffee and then to the TV to view the morning news. There was an air of dread this day. The happy days of last year were gone. The market had been behaving erratically lately. The month of September had seen the bankruptcy of Lehman Brothers, one of the too-big-to-fail banks immersed in a sea of red ink caused by the subprime mortgage mess. The government had already intervened to save Bear Stearns, another mega bank, and in July, the twin towers of home loans, Freddie Mac and Fannie Mae, had been bailed out. The market fell with every piece of news and rose with every analyst's reassurance that we were at the bottom and it had nowhere to go but up.

When John came to work that Monday, the first thing he did was turn on the office TV to catch the beginning of the Wall Street trading day. As if it were a dark omen, there were technical problems. There was no opening bell. What happened after that was all downhill. Stocks were getting hammered. By midday, the market was down 21 percent, and by the end of the day, it had lost nearly half of its value. Commentators couldn't believe what was happening. Neither could John. He had two months to go before retirement, and he was watching his fortune disappear before his eyes.

John somehow made it through the day, but all he could think about was his stake in all of this. He wondered how the activity on Wall Street would affect his retirement nest egg. He waited until five o'clock to pull up his account on his computer and assess the damage. The stock market had not behaved this badly since 1929. Five years of gains were wiped out in a single day. The DJIA had lost 777.68 points, a record. He had some side investments and a little stashed away in the bank, but most of his life's savings was in his 401(k) account. If the mutual funds that made up his 401(k) account followed suit, this could get ugly.

When John pulled up his account, he was horrified to see that he had lost over one-third of his life savings. His account that contained $1.5 million a year ago had lost over $500,000. He was devastated.

"There goes retirement," he muttered to himself.

Next day he called his stockbroker, who looked after his side investments that totaled a little over $100,000.

He asked, "What should I do?"

"Just sit tight," the broker told him. "The market goes up, and the market goes down. You know that, John. It will come back. Trust me!"

When he got home that evening, he and Jenny discussed the somber statistics of their financial situation. They were going to be okay, but the optimism of last year had turned to worry about what would happen next. It looked like they would have to make some adjustments in their plans. Perhaps Jenny's "dream folder" would have to wait a while.

"The broker said not to feel like the Lone Ranger," John told Jenny. "He said, when the tide goes out, all the boats go down, but they rise again when the tide comes back in."

"That sounds clever," Jenny replied, "but this wasn't the tide going out. This was the ocean drying up! And it couldn't have happened at a worse time, just as you were getting ready to retire."

John decided to follow the broker's advice, however, and hang in there, waiting for the ship to right itself. He told himself that a good investor has patience and doesn't let a few losses shake his foundation. In the back of his mind, he worried about what would happen if this recovery dragged its feet like the one of 1929. That recovery spanned more than twenty-five years!

For the next two weeks, John refused to look at his account. He had already decided to take his broker's advice and just "hang in there." He couldn't help but notice that, with each passing day, the news was bad. The US Labor Department reported that, in one month, the nation lost almost 160,000 jobs. On Monday, October 6, the DJIA closed below 10,000 for the first time since 2004. The Federal Reserve was lending over $500 billion to money markets to fight the nation's liquidity crisis, and more bailouts were on the way.

On the day of his retirement, John's co-workers had a little office party for him. They sang "He's a Jolly Good Fellow" and had a little cake and ice cream to celebrate his last day at work. John tried to put on a good face. It was hard because he had peeked at his 401(k) balance that morning and discovered to his horror that he had lost another $200,000. He felt envious of his younger co-workers. Many of them could afford to "hang in there" with their accounts and ride this thing out.

His wife's words kept coming back to him, "This couldn't have happened at a worse time."

His broker was not answering his telephone now. "Please leave a message," the machine said.

He left three messages before his call was finally returned. "This thing has thrown us all for a loop," the stockbroker said.

"You told me to hang in there," John said pleadingly. "How long should I hang in there until it all goes poof in the wind?" He knew he sounded frustrated, but he was frustrated and didn't know what to do. "I've just retired. Should I move everything to money market funds? Just get out while I have something left?"

"You could do that," the broker replied, "but if you do, what if the market turns around? Then you will miss out on the recovery. Look, John, I wish I could tell you what to do, but at this point, I don't know. Anything could happen."

John knew the man was just doing his job, and he had no way of knowing anything like this could happen. He didn't hold him accountable, but still he just felt rotten about this sudden turn of events.

In January 2009, it looked like the clouds were parting, and the sun was going to break through on Wall Street. The day after New Year's Day, January 2, the market rose to 9,034.69. There was a hope that the new administration in the White House could fix things. Those hopes were dashed when the market continued its tumble and found its true bottom at 6,594.44.

John was numb. He had now lost half of his life's savings, the money he had worked for more than thirty years to accumulate.

Two weeks before, John finally made the phone call to move all the money in his 401(k) to money market funds to stop the bleeding. He couldn't take a chance on losing anymore. He didn't know how long he and Jenny would live in retirement, but he was seriously worried now that they would not have enough to see them through. He pondered on when he would run out.

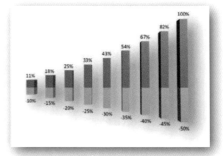

He wondered why, with all the smart people in government and on

Wall Street, there were no warning signs. When he was pumping his regular contribution into his retirement program, no one talked about market risk. When the personnel department put on their occasional dog-and-pony show about the investment choices within the 401(k), they never mentioned an exit strategy that would take such a disaster into account. It was like the *Titanic* sinking. There were no lifeboats left. It was every man for himself!

As the months went on, John discovered something else about his retirement account that people had failed to mention, at least not in any detail that he could remember – taxes. When he was putting money into his program, the taxes were postponed until later. Later was now! With every withdrawal he made from his decimated retirement account, he had to pay taxes as if he were still employed.

"It's a double whammy," he told his wife.

Understanding Market Losses

We need to have a realistic understanding of what gains and losses look like from a practical point of view. If you have a stock or any investment for that matter worth and it drops 10 percent, the value is now ninety dollars. If tomorrow, the investment is up 10 percent, are you back at even? If you calculate the 10 percent gain on ninety dollars (nine dollars), your value is now at ninety-nine dollars instead of breaking even. While this may not seem like a large difference, the distinction is much more substantial the higher the loss incurred.

In the attached chart, the bottom shows different levels of market loss, and the darker column above shows the amount of gain that you need just to break even.

To illustrate this concept differently, put four quarters on a tabletop to represent your portfolio. You lose 50 percent, so take away two quarters. Here is where it gets a little tricky.

You ask, "If I lose 50 percent, how much do I have to gain to get back to where I started?"

If the answer comes back 50 percent, slide one quarter back onto the table. That's when the light bulb clicks on.

If I give you 50 percent, you are left with three quarters. I have to give you a 100 percent gain in order to make you whole again. That makes perfect sense with quarters, yet some people have trouble grasping it with their investments in the stock market.

CHAPTER 3

THE PROBLEM WITH AVERAGES

A s soon as I hear someone selling something and he or she starts talking about averages, my radar goes up. I immediately start looking for the catch, the lie, the misdirection. To say that averages can be deceiving is like saying that the weather could change. You've heard the one about the guy with one foot in a bucket of hot water and one foot in a bucket of ice water. On average, he's comfortable.

I have heard stock brokers say, "Your investment in the stock market may be somewhat at risk, but don't worry. The market may have its ups and downs, but on average, the market has been going up 10 percent per year for the past hundred years."

That may be, but what does that really tell you?

A man might say, "My wife and I ride our bikes an average of seventy miles a week."

You form a mental picture of the two of them pedaling down the road at the crack of dawn. The truth is that she gets up at the crack of dawn every day and rides five miles out and five miles back while he sleeps in. Was the man lying? Not really. But it was deceiving, wasn't it?

People selling investments publish average statistics with the obvious inference that, when it all shakes out, you will experience the same return. I don't think they are maliciously lying. Many of them don't even grasp how misleading averages can be. But average returns and actual returns are two different things. To say "the average rate of return in this investment is 10 percent" sounds pretty good. But what about the losses and the timing of those losses?

Try this: Get out a sheet of paper, and divide it into two columns. At the top of the left column, write "50 Percent Gain." Write "50 Percent Loss" at the top of the other column. If we are calculating the average return gains and losses, it should have equal weight, correct? So we start with an average gain of zero.

Now let's put some money in this account. Start with $100,000. Write that at the top of the page in the center of the paper. Now calculate a 50 percent gain. Congratulations. You now have $150,000. Write that in the left-hand column. Now apply a 50 percent loss to the account. See what happened? Your account is now worth $75,000. You had a 50 percent gain and a 50 percent loss, both of which were equal in weight on average, but your actual return was a 25 percent loss from the original balance. When calculating actual returns, the loss had a greater impact on your pocketbook, didn't it?

What if someone made you a proposition as follows, "How would you like to have an investment that earned an average rate of return of 25 percent over two years?"

You may be inclined to jump on it, but be careful. To make the math easy, say you invested $100,000 and experienced a 100 percent return the first year. You begin the second year with $200,000. During the second year, however, you had a 50 percent loss. You're back where you started. You may have averaged a 25 percent rate of return, but your actual return was zero.

Let's say you started with $100,000, earned a 100 percent return the first year, and then had a 60 percent loss the second year. You had an average rate of return of 20 percent, but you actually lost $20,000 in the process.

Once you begin breaking down averages, it is easy to see how misleading they can become, especially factoring in negative years with a sequence of returns, as is the case with most of our investment portfolios. This is perhaps one of the reasons for Warren Buffett's two rules of investing: Rule #1: Never lose money. Rule #2: Never forget rule #1.

Sequence of Returns

As any comedian or NFL quarterback will tell you, timing is everything. When it comes to investing for retirement, the timing of a market downturn can wreak havoc on a retirement account, especially when you leave it in the stock market and flip the switch from accumulation to distribution.

During the accumulation period, the account grows, thanks to the power of dollar-cost averaging. If you are consistent with your contributions, you don't really mind when the market takes a nosedive. Your contributions are buying more shares. Time is on your side.

Once you retire, however, the opposite is true. You will probably make the same withdrawal from that account every month. Now a market downturn is a double whammy. You have to sell more shares to write yourself the same paycheck. Once the market recovers, you have less in your account to take advantage of the uptick.

There's another force at work called "sequence of returns." When a market-based retirement account is in the withdrawal (or distribution) phase, the difference between average and actual returns really matters.

The Case of the Bill and Steve

So you can time your retirement, but you can't time the markets. Returns will fall in random sequence and in varying amounts. To illustrate the impact the sequence of returns can have on individual retirement scenarios, consider the case of two brothers we will call Bill and Steve. They are fictional, of course, but the returns shown in the accompanying chart are based on actual market returns for the years indicated.

Both have $1 million in an individual retirement account (IRA) at retirement. Both will withdraw $60,000 per year for retirement income. Steve retires in 1990. Younger brother Bill follows ten years later. An interesting dynamic is at work here. The $60,000 they each withdraw is a constant. But the number the $60,000 is subtracted from keeps moving, affected each year, either positively or negatively, by the returns of the market, which are unpredictable. The timing is random.

Can you see how Steve benefits from good timing and ends up with more than twice what he started with after a ten-year period while poor Bill takes it on the chin? You can extrapolate for yourselves what a difference this makes in their lifestyle and peace of mind. Kind of stresses the value of locking in a guaranteed lifetime income, doesn't it?

Steve Retired in 1990			
Year	Return	WD	Balance
1990	-6.56%	$60,000	$874,400
1991	26.31%	$60,000	$1,044,455
1992	4.46%	$60,000	$1,031,037
1993	7.06%	$60,000	$1,043,829
1994	-1.54%	$60,000	$967,754
1995	34.11%	$60,000	$1,237,854
1996	20.26%	$60,000	$1,428,644
1997	31.01%	$60,000	$1,811,666
1998	26.67%	$60,000	$2,234,837
1999	19.53%	$60,000	$2,611,301

Bill Retired in 2000				
Year	Year	Return	WD	Balance
2000	2000	-4.24%	$60,000	$897,600
2001	2001	-12.02%	$60,000	$729,708
2002	2002	-22.15%	$60,000	$508,078
2003	2003	28.50%	$60,000	$592,880
2004	2004	10.74%	$60,000	$596,556
2005	2005	4.77%	$60,000	$565,011
2006	2006	15.64%	$60,000	$593,379
2007	2007	5.39%	$60,000	$565,362
2008	2008	-37.02%	$60,000	$296,065
2009	2009	26.49%	$60,000	$314,493

Stockbrokers like to post a thirty-year snapshot of market returns as if it accurately reflects what the market is likely to do in the next five or ten years. You can see how deceptive this is, especially to retirees. A chart of market return data from 1970 to 2010, for example, would include the bull market days of the 1980s and 1990s. If you were to flatten out the graph, the line looks good, a steady curve upward. But an entirely picture appears if you had retired just as the market took its tumble in 2008.

This is one reason why I advise clients who are averse to having their hard-earned retirement nest egg placed at an inordinate risk in retirement to consider strategies that would enable them to index the market when it is surging and lock in their gains when it recedes. That way, they never have to worry about a negative return. No matter what the market does, they know they will always be able to sleep at night. The worst they can do is zero. We have already seen how devastating losses can be to a retirement account. So, what if you could eliminate them all? And what if your account could track the gains of the stock market but not participate in the downs? It sounds like a pretty powerful strategy, doesn't it?

You Can't Time Markets

Markets, by their very nature, are unpredictable. They are like those vast storm formations at sea we call hurricanes or typhoons, depending on which part of the globe you call home. They are driven by their own forces and seem to have a mind of their own. Hurricanes confound weather forecasters who try to pinpoint where the eye of the storm will go. They can give you projections and possible paths, but those who make the predictions are often left retracting their predictions and having to explain why the darn thing floated out to sea when it was supposed to crash inland, or vice versa.

To quote the homespun humor of one market observer, "Trying to predict the market is like looking into a frog's eyes and trying to tell which way he is going to jump." I love the line from *The Economist,* a London-based financial magazine, "Stock market crashes can be like busses. You wait for ages for one to come along, then three arrive at once."

Many of my colleagues subscribe to the "random walk" theory, which states that past performance of a stock or past trends of a market cannot be used to predict its future movement. Stock charts show only the past. You can analyze them until you are blue in the face, and you still won't know the future. It's like trying to predict a meandering path, or a "random walk."

I am continuously amused at the fund managers who advertise themselves as stock market gurus who have some kind of prescient instinct. "Give me your money, and let me pick the stocks that will give you the best return on your money."

Let's get real. If they could actually pick stocks they knew would do well and reject stocks they knew would perform poorly, wouldn't they already have done it for themselves? Wouldn't they already have enriched themselves with this special gift? They would have all the money in the world. Game over. So it's an investing myth on the same order of the flat earth theory.

Not even the CEOs of giant corporations know what their profits are going to be from one quarter to the next. How could a stock picker possibly have that information and beat them to the market with it? Besides that, world events can change in a heartbeat, affecting the markets in the same instant. If such unknowables are factored into stock prices, it defies logic to think one could see those consequences before they happen.

There are also those who would like for you to believe that they don't have this gift of picking stocks, but they work for a company with a lot of really smart people at the home office who do have the aptitude. If you just let them manage your money, you will get the benefit of these seers. To make the point, they point to a fund manager's track record of having "beat the market" three years in a row.

Let's think about that one. Have you ever noticed just how many mutual funds there are in the world? There are thousands of them! At last count, there are over seven thousand in the United States alone. Sure, a handful are able to beat the market for a few consecutive years, but the vast majority can't and don't. And after a while, we don't hear from them again. They are absorbed into other funds or simply disappear. So pointing to that handful as proof that they can outperform the market is using the illusion of hindsight bias.

What if you stood a thousand people in a room, gave each a coin, and had everyone flip his or her coin. You tell those whose coin came up heads to remain standing and the others to sit down. According to the law of averages, half would take a seat, and the other half would remain standing. If you repeat this ten times, you may have ten people standing at the end. Does that mean that those who were left standing were experts in physics and had some kind of sixth sense as to just what pressure they should use when releasing their thumb to flip the coin? Did they figure out some scientific formula for how many revolutions the coin would need to make in the air in order to land heads up? Did they do some calculation that measured the weight of the coin and factored in the resistance of the surface of the coin against the atmosphere in the room? No, they just got lucky.

So to take a handful of fund managers who beat the market a few consecutive times in a row and lift them to the status of omniscience is ludicrous. The idea they have some special knowledge is an illusion.

CHAPTER 4

WHY BUY-AND-HOLD NO LONGER WORKS

I saw a clever cartoon strip the other day. There were two panes: one marked "1950" and the other marked "Today." In the 1950 pane, a man stood dressed in a hat and a suit, holding what was obviously a certificate of some sort. He was saying, "I'll pass these stocks along to the children."

In the adjoining pane, a man is seated at a computer. He says to his wife, we assume, who is not in the frame, "Honey, do you want to hold this trade over the weekend?"

To which she replies, "No! Too risky!"

That little slice of humor well illustrates that, when it comes to investing, times have changed. Buy-and-hold is an investment strategy where an investor buys stocks and holds them for a long time. There may have been a time in America when you could purchase shares in a few mutual funds and just sit back and watch them grow like a tomato garden, but that was back in the days when the stock market was predictable and you could depend on a steady rhythm of advances and retreats, similar to ocean tides. But that's just not the case lately. Since the twenty-first century began, the stock market has behaved much too erratically, but long-term set-it-and-forget-it investing. It is not without reason that people call the stock market a roller-coaster ride. It is volatile and unpredictable.

Any market floats on perceived value and is subject to the mood of its buyers and sellers. Financial markets are no different. Years ago, a corporation's long-term earnings governed the value of its publicly held shares. But now, with computer trading and instant news from around the world beamed in on our smartphones, current events and the protean mood of jittery investors greatly influences the stock market. A political disturbance somewhere two oceans away is instantly registered on our hemisphere, prompting markets to react with lightning speed. When trading is done on computers, milliseconds can make an enormous difference. It is foolish to even think that, in today's investing environment, you could establish a position in the market, check on it once a year, and expect your portfolio to remain intact. And yet that is what many books, magazine articles, and brokerage people will tell you.

When the market tanks, their mantra is, "Just hold on. Don't panic. Ride it out. Hang in there. Keep the faith. It will come back."

Stockbroker types may like to play that as their theme music while their clients' portfolios are bleeding and Wall Street is begging for bailouts, but it is not very soothing to those whose life's savings are disappearing. And professional traders use complex tools that were unavailable in the 1990s, not to mention the influence of hedge funds, derivatives, and the manipulative influence of the Federal Reserve.

The idea behind the buy-and-hold strategy is that markets will always come back in a matter of months. And it's not just that they will come back in a timely fashion. They will come back to the point where they crashed, exceed that mark, and make new highs. Is that always the case? Not always. It is true that, for every market downturn, there is always a market recovery. This undulation is the very nature of a market.

But as previously pointed out in this book, timing is everything when investing is involved. Those on the threshold of retirement may not have time to benefit from a market recovery that takes its sweet time. For them, using a buy-and-hold strategy is tantamount to playing with a loaded revolver.

[3]What does history teach us about market recoveries? The longest domestic recovery on record is the twenty-five years it took for the American stock market to recover from the crash of 1929 and the ensuing Great Depression. I know that some market analysts like to dismiss

---

3 (Kelly, Patrick. *The Retirement Miracle*. United States: Bluewater, 2011. Print.)

that statistic by pointing out that deflation and other factors weren't included in the calculation. But even if you could shave three or four years off that quarter century, that is a long time, practically the working life of a generation to wait for the market to come back while you just "sat tight, held on, didn't panic, and rode it out."

The worst of the worst example of how long it can take for a market to recover is the Japanese Nikkei. Maybe you remember when Japanese nationals were buying up golf courses and resort hotels in America in the late 1980s because, based on the value of the yen over the dollar, everything was on sale. The Japanese is the third-largest economy in the world behind the United States and China. On December 29, 1989, the Nikkei 225, the counterpart to the DJIA in the United States, was on a roll, peaking at 38,957.

Twenty years later, investors were still waiting for the big comeback, and the value of the Nikkei was at 73 percent below that high-water mark. From the looks of things, the Japanese stock market will break the record of the US stock market for the longest recovery period ever. As I write this, the Nikkei is flirting with 18,000. Alex Planes, writing in December 29, 2012 article, "Bear Market Without End," published in *The Motley Fool*, an online investing magazine, said, "This market may come back given enough time, but it will be too late to save a generation of potential Japanese investors that have watched the Nikkei slide for their entire adult lives."

Let's see now. How did the buy-and-hold strategy work out for those Japanese investors in the 1990s? It didn't. If they held on, sat tight, remained patient, and rode it out, they would still be watching their assets dwindle. Can we learn anything from the Nikkei? I certainly hope so. As the old saying goes, "Those who cannot learn from the past are doomed to repeat it."

In *The Retirement Miracle*, Patrick Kelly compares the value of $1,000 in the Nikkei as of December 1989 with what it would be worth twenty years hence in 2009, $271.01. He makes the point that, even though the total return through the end of 2009 is a negative 73.8 percent, nine of the individual years in the two decades prior to 2009 produced positive returns. He cites 2005 as an example when the Nikkei index rose an encouraging 40.24 percent. The only problem was that 2007 and 2008 took it all back and then some.[3]

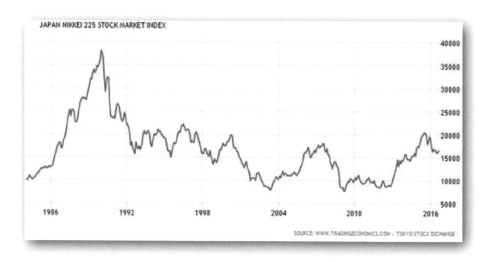

In this graph of the Nikkei showing returns from 1984 to 2016, if you invested $10,000 in 1984, it would have grown to almost $40,000 by 1990. Thirty-two years later, in 2016, your original $10,000 would be worth just over $17,000.

So What Now?

[4]Can you see why I say that buy-and-hold as an investing strategy has gone the way of the dinosaur and rotary dial telephones? Looking at the historical returns of the Nikkei is a good reminder that there is no law stating that the markets will always turn around on the long term. But if buy-and-hold strategies don't work, what about an active trading strategy?

Recently, Brad Barber of UC Davis and Terrance Odean of UC Berkeley released research that concluded that only about 1 percent of active traders outperformed the market. It's not entirely the trader's fault either. Trading costs and management fees often eat up a majority of the additional gains that an active trader is able to achieve.[4]

What if, instead of taking a buy-and-hold strategy or an active trader stance, we did something very different? What if we take out all the years with losses and make them zeroes? Then we put a limit or cap of 12 percent on all the years where there was a gain. How do you think that would perform?

4   (Barber, Brad M., and Terrance Odean. "The Behavior of Individual Investors." *Handbook of the Economics of Finance* (2013): 1533-570. Web. 29 Dec. 2016.)

The chart below shows an initial investment of $500,000 at the beginning of one of the worst stock market runs in history (2000–2016) compared to the performance of the S&P 500. Over that sixteen-year time frame this indexed strategy, as we call it, tripled in value to $1,572,031.

What would have happened if you were fully invested in the S&P 500? Your account value would have doubled, and be worth $1,058,177. The indexed account increased more than $500k over the S&P 500! Sounds too good to be true, right? That is the power of eliminating the losses from the picture. That's right. If the market zoomed up 40 percent one year, let's say, just whittle that increase down to 12 percent. Make any year where the market went down a zero, and it is amazing what a difference it makes to the investor.

Why bring that up? These indexing strategies are available, and they enable ordinary investors to have that type of return to capture each year where there is a gain and lock in that gain. You thus make zero your hero by eliminating losses. It is available, and it is probably one of the best-kept secrets of the investing world.

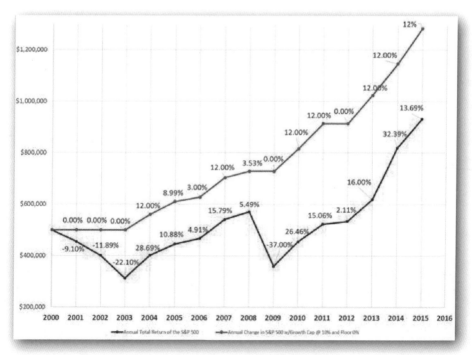

In the above illustration, eliminating losses and locking in all gains, the difference is amazing. The bottom line is the annual total returns of the S&P between 2000 and 2016, and the top line is an indexed account with a growth cap of 12 percent and a floor of zero. As the table below indicates, $500,000 invested in an indexed account in 2000 becomes $1,572,025 at the end of 2016.

Year	S&P 500 Return	Value	S&P500 Return w/growth cap	Value
2000		$500,000		$500,000
2001	-9.10%	$454,500	0.00%	$500,000
2002	-11.89%	$400,459	0.00%	$500,000
2003	-22.10%	$311,958	0.00%	$500,000
2004	28.69%	$401,459	12.00%	$560,000
2005	10.88%	$445,137	8.99%	$610,344
2006	4.91%	$466,994	3.00%	$628,654
2007	15.79%	$540,732	12.00%	$704,092
2008	5.49%	$570,418	3.53%	$728,947
2009	-37.00%	$359,363	0.00%	$728,947
2010	26.46%	$454,451	12.00%	$816,420
2011	15.06%	$522,891	12.00%	$914,391
2012	2.11%	$533,924	0.00%	$914,391
2013	16.00%	$619,352	12.00%	$1,024,118
2014	32.39%	$819,961	12.00%	$1,147,012
2015	13.69%	$932,213	12.00%	$1,284,654

A Case for Safe Money Investing

As a financial advisor specializing in retirement planning, I saw first-hand the human cost of the 2008 financial meltdown. Our firm works primarily with those approaching retirement and those already retired. Thankfully, because our firm believes in safe money investing and wealth preservation, the 2008 market crash did not hurt any of my clients. But the losses experienced by some who sought our services after the crash were heartrending indeed.

One couple told me how they had lost nearly half their life savings in the crash. She was a nurse, and he owned a small construction business. Both were hard workers and savers.

"Our mistake was just not paying enough attention," said the woman tearfully.

They had apparently parked their savings with a big brokerage house and allowed the people behind the desks in the glass tower buildings make investment decisions for them. When the market started to slide, they had more than $700,000, all invested in mutual funds, stocks, bonds, and variable annuities. Once they saw the Wall Street debacle plundering their nest egg, their broker advised them to stay put, saying the market would rebound.

"The problem is," said the man, "we don't have time for it to rebound. I had maybe one more year before I retired, and she had maybe a year and a half. We were planning to live on that money, and now half of it is gone, and I'm worried about the other half."

"That's fine for younger people," she said. "We don't have time to wait for it to rebound."

Their home was paid for. Once they retired, they had planned to sell their home, buy a smaller one in the mountains near a lake, and use a portion of the equity remaining to purchase a motor home. They wanted to travel. They lost more than $60,000 equity when the housing bubble burst. They had to postpone their retirement and continue working.

The financial trauma experienced by this couple was typical of many. In one seminar I conducted shortly after the market tumble, I observed that many were downright angry. They had put their trust in institutions they thought were rock-solid. They had entrusted their fortunes to professionals who claimed to be working in their best interests.

"Why didn't anyone see this coming?" asked one man in frustration.

I thought the answer but did not say it. It was, after all, a rhetorical question. While no human could have predicted the housing bubble, the market crash, or the Great Recession that followed, there are those who have all along advocated safe money investing with guaranteed returns. It's just that, when the economy is booming, the voice of reason is difficult to hear. No one could have predicted every turn of the downward spiral in the credit crisis, but there always were those who warned against having too much money at risk as you approach retirement. Even the brightest on Wall Street couldn't connect the dots among the housing bubble, mortgage defaults, and bank and stock market collapses. But there have always been those who have warned that anything that looks too good to be true usually is.

Making Adjustments

To use a sailing metaphor, "You can't change the wind, but you can adjust your sails." We didn't ask for the prevailing market volatility, but it does no good to pretend like it doesn't exist and invest like our parents did in the 1950s. Trying to time the market is like trying to anticipate which way a coin will land when flipped. You may get it right five times in a row, but that doesn't mean you controlled it. The odds are still 50/50. The next five calls may just prove that to you too.

The market is its own entity. We can study it all we want, but we will not change it. What we can modify, however, is our approach to investing once the old approach is outdated and ineffective. We can abandon investing methods that no longer work and then employ and adhere to the ones that do.

In the current investing environment, flexibility is the key. There is no one-and-only right way in today's economic climate. The more education we possess about the economy and the movement of its markets, the better we can plan. The difference between the investors who lost as much as half of their life's savings in the financial crisis of 2008 and those who lost very little or nothing at all was that some were able to see and understand what others could not.

The old expression, "knowledge is power," isn't quite accurate. A high school class was asked to write a report defining three words—knowledge, wisdom, and understanding—and then explain the difference.

"Knowledge," one student wrote, "is a collection of data and an accumulation of facts that you learn about something. Knowledge is information obtained through experience, observation, study, and research."

"Understanding," she wrote, "is insight. It is grasping the perception of what we know and seeing what the facts really mean and how they relate to each other."

"Wisdom," she concluded, "is the ability to discern and judge which aspects of our collection of knowledge are applicable to our lives and applying the knowledge in a way that is beneficial to our well-being."

The teacher gave her an A. The best grade, however, an A-plus, went to a boy in the class who put it this way, "Knowledge is when you are standing on a railroad track and know the train is coming. Understanding is getting it in your head what the train will do to your body if it hits you. Wisdom is getting off the tracks."

Of course, knowledge is power, but only if we take the appropriate action.

CHAPTER 5

A Brief History of Indexed Universal Life (IUL)

I n the previous chapter, I pointed out how huge it is to eliminate losses and how great it would be to have a product that would enable the average investor to capture the positive gains of the stock market each year, up to a reasonable cap, while at the same time eliminate losses, period. Hold on to your armrest, fellow investor. That product is indexed universal life (IUL) insurance.

As soon as you mention insurance, a flood of mental pictures comes across the mind, and not all of them are positive. Life insurance is boring. It is one of those necessary things that almost every person has but no one wants to think about, let alone explore as an exciting investment product. But I'm not talking about your grandfather's life insurance policy here. Unless you have kept up with the developments of insurance as a viable investment tool lately, you probably know very little about IUL. Let me start at the beginning.

The Birth and Development of IUL

Humans are smart enough to put a man on the moon, but they have so far been unable to figure out a way to keep from dying. Life insurance was invented to help people offset the financial consequences of that eventuality. In ancient Rome, soldiers got together and formed a burial club so, if they fell in battle, they would get a decent burial and their families back home would be cared for. It was the first example in recorded history of pooling resources. The Romans believed, without a ceremonial burial, the dead would become unhappy and haunt their loved ones. The government later picked up the idea and made it part of the military benefits package.

The insurance concept sort of fell by the wayside during the Dark Ages and reappeared in seventeenth-century England when Sir Edmund Halley (yes, the guy after whom the comet is named) came up with a way to make it into a business. Halley, mathematical genius, loved tinkering with numbers when he wasn't staring at the heavens through a telescope. Halley was curious about the statistics associated with human mortality. His research in this field led him to the Polish city of Breslau, now Wroclaw, that kept detailed records of when people were born and when they died.

In 1693, he published his findings in an article, "An Estimate of the Degrees of the Mortality of Mankind." He came up with a mathematical formula that insurance companies would use for hundreds of years to determine how much they could charge for a life insurance policy and still make a profit. It all still hinged on two things: the law of large numbers and human life expectancy.[5]

Advance the clock to the late 1970s. Inflation was spiraling out of control. Jimmy Carter was president, not that he had much to do with the double-digit interest rates rapid-fire wage and price hikes. His predecessors had caused the problems over which it was his dubious honor to preside. It was an interesting time. Men were wearing polyester leisure suits, and miniskirts were all the rage. Early baby boomers were just starting to come of age financially. Their hippie days were behind them, and they were becoming responsible citizens with jobs and mortgages. They were also in the market for life insurance.

But something was very wrong with the policies that insurance companies were offering in the late 1970s. Interest rates down at the bank were in double digits, yet traditional whole life insurance policies were paying only 1 or 2 percent on the cash value portion of the contract. Financially speaking, times were changing, and insurance companies

---

5   http://cerebro.xu.edu/math/Sources/Halley/halley.html

were stuck in the 1950s, paying an arbitrary low percentage of interest as they had always done. Nothing in the regulations or bylaws governing insurance companies required them to disclose the inner workings of their policies to policyholders, so they didn't.

But that didn't cut it with this new generation of consumers. They voted with their pocketbooks and started cashing in their whole life policies by the thousands, opting for higher interest rates paid by banks. They bought cheaper term policies to replace the death benefits of traditional whole life policies. "Buy term and invest the difference" was a concept sweeping the nation, and insurance companies were forced to pay attention and reinvent themselves. An insurance revolution was taking place. The fact that a Federal Trade Commission (FTC) investigation of whole life insurance probably served to accelerate matters somewhat.

A few forward-thinking insurance companies put their product design people in a room with their actuaries and ordered them to come up with a solution, a relatively new concept called "universal life," or UL, that called for flexibility and transparency. Interest on cash value policies would no longer be arbitrary but would be pegged to US Treasury bills. In 1982, T-Bills were paying an attractive 14.59 percent. This was public knowledge. Policyholders could easily keep track of their returns on a daily basis if they wished, simply by checking the newspaper or calling the insurance company.

Flexible? UL premiums were whatever you wanted them to be. You could pump up the cash value by overpaying the premiums, or you could pay the minimum, just enough to cover the death benefit. You could even skip premiums if you needed to and let the cash value pay them for you. Policyholders could even make withdrawals from their cash value with low-interest loans. UL premiums were quite flexible too. Consumers had the option to pay more into the policy during feast and pay less or even skip premiums during famine. Death benefits remained tax-free, and policyholders could even make withdrawals in the form of low-interest loans.

UL was clawing its way back, gaining back some of its share of the consumer market, extending ground it had lost to the buy-term-and-invest-the-difference movement. Things were looking up for the insurance industry. Interest rates were off their double-digit peaks, but they remained relatively high throughout the 1980s. Just when it seemed that the itch had been scratched, the prime rate dropped from 10.87 percent in 1989 to 6 percent in 1994. The drop in T-Bills diminished some of the appeal of UL policies, so it was back to the ol' drawing board. The result was a new wrinkle on that would come to be known as indexed universal life (IUL).

Introduced in 1997, IUL featured a new method of crediting interest to the cash value of policies. The idea was to peg returns to the upward movement of a stock market index, such as the S&P 500, while retaining such desirable characteristics as flexibility of premiums and an adjustable face value (death benefit). Policyholders could even juice up the earning capacity of the policy by overfunding, that is, pouring more into the policy than was required to cover the death benefit.

The insurance industry pegged this new type of policy as investment-grade life insurance because now individuals could benefit from a surging stock market without being negatively affected by its downside. There were some glitches to work out, however.

At first, investors could pump as much as they wanted into these policies. So what's wrong with that? Nothing, as far as the policy owner was concerned. The cash value grew tax-deferred and could be removed tax-free. Uncle Sam wasn't too happy with that arrangement, however. The IRS soon plugged that loophole with new laws that would limit the amount you could invest in IUL policies by introducing the acronym sisters: Tax, Equity, Fiscal and Responsibility Act of 1982 (TEFRA), Deficit Reduction Act of 1984 (DEFRA), and Technical and Miscellaneous Revenue Act of 1988 (TAMRA).

Without boring you to tears with the details, in one way or another, these regulations curbed abuse of the tax-free provisions of IUL. But fortunately they left intact the provisions that allowed investors to benefit from bull markets (surging market) and remain protected during bear markets (falling market).

How would this new product be received? American consumers are well known for their fickle nature. Would they pluck IUL from the shelves, recognizing it as a way to have safety of principal and generate a tax-free retirement? Or would they eschew it because it had a few moving parts? Would they embrace this new insurance technology the same way they had the personal computer? Or would they pass it by? Time would tell.

CHAPTER 6

INDEXED UNIVERSAL LIFE (IUL): FEATURES AND BENEFITS

W hen IUL was introduced in 1997, it was unclear how it would be received. After all, this was something new and different. The American public is well known for voting with its pocketbook. If John Q. Public doesn't want or like something, all the advertising and sales promotion in the world won't make it catch on. The Edsel and New Coke are two good examples of that.

But this new approach seemed to hit the spot finally with the great American buying public. It was a product whose time had come, and from the statistics, it appears that IULs were very well received. According to insurance researcher LIMRA, IUL is the fastest-growing type of life insurance on the market, having grown 192 percent from 2006–2010. As I write this, over fifty insurance companies now offer IUL contracts. Like I said, Americans always vote with their wallets.

People who know me recognize that I put everything under a microscope. I have looked very closely at this product, and I can't find any holes in it. Compared to its predecessor, whole life insurance, IUL insurance is like comparing a fine chronograph watch to a sundial. Along with the increased functionality comes a few more moving parts.

These investment-grade policies are financial instruments. It is easier to describe what they do than it is to describe how they do it. That's why I suggest you work with professional advisors who can explain their inner workings to your satisfaction. Without getting too complicated, here is an overview:

- **The Tax-Free Death Benefit:** At the core of every life insurance policy is the death benefit, and that is as it should be. Ask any family where the breadwinner died prematurely and those left behind were able to continue the same living standard as before because of life insurance. With IUL policies, that cornerstone is still at the heart of the contract. Unique among IRS laws is the statute that provides for death benefits to be income tax-free. Part of the IUL premium pays for the raw insurance feature of the policy, which essentially functions like annual renewable term life. The coverage is based on the age and health of the one who is insured. This part is funded first, and what is left over is added to the policy's cash value. People who use an IUL insurance policy for a tax-free retirement can overfund the policy and thereby accelerate the cash growth.
- **Cash Value Accumulation:** This is where IUL really shines, if you ask me. Most cash value life insurance policies have this feature, the potential for cash accumulation within the contract. But the horsepower of this new breed of insurance is beyond anything ever put out before because it tracks the upward movement of the stock market. The cash value in the policy can be used at the discretion of the policy owner by making a tax-free withdrawal up to the total amount of premiums he or she has paid into the policy. The withdrawal merely represents a return of the after-tax money that the policy owner originally contributed to the policy.
- **No Market Losses:** The IUL contract guarantees that your cash value can never lose value because of a stock market downturn. That is huge! Anyone who has ever made money in the stock market remembers how sweet those periods are when everything goes up, up, up. But there is always that uneasiness with every run-up that storm clouds are gathering somewhere and there will be a crash. During the 2008 market crash, for example, people lost as much as half their life savings in the market. Those who were growing their money as cash value in an IUL policy suffered

37

none of those losses. The trade-off, of course, is that, with an IUL, you have a cap on your earnings. In other words, if the market zooms up twenty points, you will be capped at, say, fifteen or sixteen. But who wouldn't make that trade-off to make sure he or she would never have a losing year? So this bears a little explaining. You are not invested directly in the stock market with an IUL. If you were, you would have to take the losses when the market goes down. Instead, the interest credited to your cash value is based on or linked to the upward (and only the upward) movement of a stock market index, such as the NASDAQ, the S&P 500, or the DJIA. Different carriers have a variety of methods for doing this. They could use a combination of these stock market indexes. Most IUL contracts offer a guaranteed minimum fixed interest rate. Most carriers allow the policyholder to have input on the crediting method. For example, they may choose to have their cash value pegged entirely to the stock market index or option to have a portion of it linked to a fixed interest strategy. Interest is usually credited to the cash account annually on the anniversary date of the policy.

- **The Ratchet/Reset Provision:** In machinery, a ratchet is the gear part that allows movement in only one direction. Socket wrenches work this way. They can turn freely in one direction, but a ratchet mechanism in the head of the wrench prevents movement the other way. Let's say the cash value in an IUL policy increases by 8 percent one year. That amount is now secure and cannot be lost if the market decides to go south the next. The ratchet effect dictates that the policy owner gets to keep whatever the cash value grows to each year, and that is the new base for cash growth. All contributions to the cash value are locked in on an annual basis. If the markets go down in a given year, your annual reset will begin from that lower value. Because of this, IUL contracts tend to perform well in up and sideways markets, where the index moves up and down from year to year, as the annual reset will lock in the gains.

- **Growth Potential:** What's the point of investing in anything if there is no potential for growth? There is none. But can you expect growth if you are protected from losses in an IUL? Absolutely! The cap, limit, or ceiling on growth will vary from company to company, but it allows for plenty of growth up to that cap. Let's say your policy is tracking the S&P 500, and it records a gain of 10 percent. If your cap is 13 percent, you get the full 10 percent credited to your cash account. If the index records an 18 percent gain one year, then what is your gain? That's right, 13 percent. One of the best parts is that the worst you can do if the market tanks is zero.

- **Tax-Deferred Growth:** Cash value grows tax-deferred, not tax-free. If you let the policy lapse prematurely, you may create a taxable event. Can you withdraw all of your funds or cancel your policy? Of course you can, but Uncle Sam will have his hand out for the taxes he is due. If you cancel a policy after many years, the amount over what you paid in premiums will be subject to income tax, not capital gains tax. There is, however, a way to access what amounts to a cash value withdrawal all together tax-free.

- **Policy Loan Provisions:** Loans—car, home, and so forth—aren't taxed. When these policies were designed, the insurance companies built a provision into them that will allow the owner the privilege of borrowing from the cash value tax-free through policy loans. But wait a minute! Aren't I borrowing my own money? In a way you are, and this is the key to using the power of an IUL to create a tax-free income. Stay tuned. I will explain this in full detail a little later on.

- **Flexible Qualifiers:** With some tax-deferred retirement savings plans, such as IRAs and simplified employee pension (SEP) accounts, there is a minimum age. Not with IULs. The policy owner is not necessarily the insured. That means, if you have an insurable interest in someone, such as a child, grandchild, or other relative, you may own a policy and overfund it for tax-deferred growth.

- **No Required Minimum Distributions (RMDs):** When you put money into a tax-qualified retirement plan, such as a 401(k) or an IRA, you will have what are called required minimum distributions (RMDs) when you reach age seventy and a half. Whether you need to withdraw the money or not, the government will force you to do so, so Uncle Sam can recoup a portion of the taxes. There are no RMDs with IUL policies. You decide when you wish to remove your money and what you want to do with it.

- **No Withdrawal Age:** You know how it works with your retirement account at work, your 401(k) plan. If you withdraw money prior to age fifty-nine and a half, you will pay a penalty of 10 percent. There's no such thing with IULs.

- **Probate and Creditor Protected:** I love this feature, especially for high-income professionals such as doctors and attorneys. In many states, the cash value that accumulates inside an insurance policy is legally protected from creditors, bankruptcies, lawsuits, and judgments. Those in the medical profession can have unwanted exposure to malpractice suits, for example. It is usually important to them for their investments to be beyond the grasp of such proceedings. Also, because your cash value is parked inside an insurance contract, it is typically immune from probate, a legal process that can delay the transfer of an estate by months or even years. The death benefit from a life insurance policy is usually paid to the beneficiary within days of the death of the insured.

- **Disability Waivers:** With IULs, an optional feature called "waiver of premium for disability" simply keeps paying your premiums for you if you become permanently disabled. Yes, I realize that is nothing new. Most all life insurance policies offer some form of protection like this. But what makes it unique with IUL policies is that this waiver, at a very reasonable additional cost, will continue to fund the policy at the current rate of contribution up to a certain level. It's like an auto-continuation provision of your regular monthly contribution in the event you become permanently disabled.

- **Does Not Count Toward Social Security Taxation:** With the IRS, income from investment accounts and CDs can be just enough to kick your Social Security into the category of 50 percent, even 85 percent, taxation. It's the same way with income from 401(k)s and SEPs. Income derived from cash value withdrawal from a life insurance policy does not fall into that category, however, and will not subject your Social Security check to taxation.

Not bad, huh? And in the interests of full disclosure, here are some bullet points you need to be aware of when considering IUL:

- You don't have to be the insured in order to own an IUL, but you must have an insurable interest in the insured.
- If you are the insured, you must be healthy enough to qualify for coverage, and you will likely be required to take a medical exam before your application is approved.
- The cash value can be used to pay the insurance premiums if necessary.
- The younger you are, the better it is when it comes to cash growth opportunity. Why? Because less of your premium is going to cover the cost of the death benefit and more is used for the cash value portion of the contract.

That is a lot of information, I know. I may not have included every little detail, but as an item-by-item rundown, that's pretty comprehensive. I think you can see why IUL is unique and why I like the project as an income-generating investment vehicle. I am not the only one, however.

What Ed Slott Says

If you watch public television, you probably know Ed Slott, one of America's most prominent and often-quoted authorities on retirement income planning in general and IRAs in particular. He has become a regular feature on PBS channel and is known for unbiased and forthright opinions. Here is what he had to say during one telecast about IUL:

> As a tax advisor, I'm advising you to take advantage of the single biggest benefit in the tax code, and that is the tax exemption for life insurance…Most people think of life insurance as something that pays off after you're dead. That's true! But what if I told you that you can have tax-free access to your life insurance during

your lifetime. You could use it for yourself. You could be moving large amounts of money from taxable accounts to a tax-free permanent life insurance policy where the money grows tax-free inside the policy.

Slott also asked the audience the following rhetorical question, "Why would you keep money growing in a taxable account when it could be transferred to a tax-free investment?"

"If you have taxable IRA funds, you can, in effect, convert your IRA to life insurance," he said.

The way Slott sees it, paying tax now at low rates on distributions from your IRA and then using that money to fund your life insurance investment accomplishes three things: reducing future tax exposure in your IRA by taking distributions now, building up a tax-free source of retirement funds should you need them, and providing your heirs with a tax-free death benefit.

"If it turns out that you don't need to tap into your life insurance investment for retirement income," Slott says, "then the life insurance benefit builds for your family income-tax free. And for most people, it will be estate tax-free too, depending on the estate tax exemption level."

Which Way Will the Stock Market Go?

I used to have a paperweight on my desk at the offices of Wealth Planning Network that looked very much like a crystal ball. It was one of those freebies from a trade show I attended years ago. It's gone now, probably the victim of desk organization. But I miss the darn thing. When someone would ask me that immortal question, "Which way do you think the market will go?" just to get a laugh (and make a point), I would gaze into the glass globe, move my hands the way fortune-tellers do, and say, "Let me see what my crystal ball says."

The fact is no one knows which way the stock market is going to go. What is downright amusing is when stockbrokers, mutual fund managers, or analysts in the media pretend to be market clairvoyants and issue predictions. What is not so funny is when people lose thousands of dollars by following their advice.

One of the most egregious examples of such behavior takes place on one of the financial channels on cable TV. A guy comes out with his sleeves rolled up while wearing a party hat. He's blowing a zoom whistle and ringing a cow bell. He is a market analyst who takes call-in questions and advises people whether to buy, sell, or hold individual stocks. I suppose his clownish behavior is supposed to get our attention, and that part of the show works. It would be easy to laugh it all off as entertainment if it weren't for the fact he is deadly serious.

Back during the 2008 financial meltdown, a viewer asked, "Should I be worried about Bear Stearns and get my money out of there?"

It was a legitimate question because the venerable, old investment bank was going under, saddled by the weight of the subprime mortgage mess.

Party Hat Boy went ballistic. He screamed at the camera, "No, no, no! Bear Stearns is fine! Do not take your money out of there!"

He was wrong, of course. The problem with hacks like him is that sometimes they guess right and people start believing they actually can see into the future.

Predictably Unpredictable

If you want a prediction, okay, I'll give you one. I predict, in the foreseeable future, the market will do one of three things: go up on some days, be down on other days, and go sideways on some days. When all is said and done, it will remain predictably unpredictable.

When I was a kid, I remember the occasional trip over to Riverview Park to ride The Bobs, an old, wooden roller coaster. At that age, few things were more exciting than being hoisted eighty-seven feet into the air and then dropped in a virtual free fall. After gravity finally overcame the momentum of the car and it coasted to a stop, my pals and I would get off and line up for another ride. We couldn't get enough of the thrills that noisy, old roller coaster could dish out.

Riverview Amusement Park was torn down in 1967. I don't think they make roller coasters out of wood like that anymore. They don't even build amusement parks anymore. Today they are called "theme parks."

The last time I was at such a park was when the kids were young enough to enjoy thrill rides. I was happy just to watch. I had no interest getting thrown around, and I noticed I was not alone. Plenty of parents and grandparents were standing around, watching the action, but none lined up to ride.

It's the same way with the stock market. That financial roller coaster ride favors young investors much more than older ones. Why? When you are young, time is on your side. Long recovery periods follow some bear markets, and young investors have time to take advantage of them. Older investors, however, could lose a significant portion of their life savings if they were forced to retire at the bottom of a stock market dip and use their nonrenewable resources to fund their lifestyle.

Obviously, if you could see into the future and knew for certain that the market would soar high for the next year or so, it would be foolish not to put as much money as you could into it. Since we can't possibly know that, it is foolish to put all of your money in the stock market on a hunch as to what it might do.

By the same token, if you could see the future and knew for certain that the market was going to head south, it would be a smart thing to either sell short or get out. Take your money, and buy real estate or gold, anything but shares of stock that you know will continue going down.

What about a sideways market? People who follow the movement of the stock market call the decade of 2000 "the lost decade." Why? The market rose and fell, as markets do, but in the end, there was much activity and little accomplishment. If you had started with $100,000 at the beginning of the decade, you would have approximately $100,000 at the end of the ten years.

How Would an IUL Perform?

So how would the cash value of an IUL policy perform in an extended sideways market? Would its returns be static as well? Not at all! Remember, a sideways market doesn't mean a flat line on the graph. It means the market is up one year and down the next. Up two years and steeply down the next, erasing all the gains. The way an IUL behaves, as it follows the trail left by the stock market index, you get a gain. The gain locks in. The market has a loss; you don't participate in that loss.

For example, let's take a ten-year sideways market and use $100,000 as your starting balance. And just for easy math, let's say the market goes up 10 percent one year and down 10 percent the next. Your $100,000 would increase to $110,000 the first year, sit on the bench in year two, and then earn another 10 percent in year three, putting you at $121,000. In year four, your money sits on the sidelines, waiting out the loss, and then enjoys another 10 percent gain in year five, putting your account value at $133,000. At the end of the decade, the five years of gains and no losses would place your account value at $161,000.

What would have happened if you had invested the same amount in an index fund? That's right! You would have ended the 10-year period with a loss! Your $100,000 would now be $95,100, or about 4.9 percent down.

I can see the gears turning right now. You're right! Each time you lost money, you had less money in the game the following year to take advantage of the gain. Can you see why we say that eliminating the losses is huge? It's a little like that roller-coaster ride. The undulating tracks of The Bobs roller coaster rose and fell as the cars went around the track, but the peaks and valleys were a little less pronounced as the ride progressed and the momentum of the cars slowed.

As mentioned earlier, percentages and averages can be tricky. A very simple way to remember this is the "four quarters" illustration. You start with four quarters on the table. I take 50 percent (two quarters) off the table, leaving you with 50 cents. I put 50 percent (one quarter) back on the table. You now have three quarters.

Because the IUL strategy never experiences a negative return, your account is producing a gain even in a sideways market! Think about that. I mean really think about that. Zero is your hero in a declining market.

Keep in mind, the illustrations I presented here involved round numbers for easy math and is not to be interpreted as an official insurance illustration by any stretch. It also doesn't include the mention of any of the working parts of the policy that involve such things as management expenses, sales charges, or raw cost of the insurance. The essence of the example given here is that avoiding losses is huge and IUL thrives even in a sideways stock market.

A Look under the Hood of IUL

As a kid, I remember helping my father work on our family car. I was no mechanic, but I understood in general how it worked. In those days, car engines didn't have computers. What was under the hood was straight-forward. It's a different story with today's automobiles, however. They are much too complex for me to even think about tinkering on. If something doesn't work right, I take it to the dealership and let them deal with it. They hook it up to the master computer, and it makes a quick diagnosis.

Modern insurance policies have more moving parts than the policies of yesteryear too. As I said earlier, it's easier to describe what they do than it is to explain how they do it. But when people hear you can share in the gains of the stock market without participating in market losses, the first thing that crosses their mind is, "How can they do that?" So let's pull the hood latch, and look at what drives IUL and learn what makes this unique feature possible.

Options, Puts, and Calls

Let's start with terms. The financial world has its own jargon, a variety of terms that may seem like a foreign language at first. The following are some investing terms you will encounter when learning what makes IULs tick:

- **Option:** In everyday language, an option is a choice. But what is the purpose of the investing tool by the same name? It too is a choice. In investing parlance, an option is a contract that gives the buyer the right (but not the obligation) to sell or buy an asset or instrument at a specified time and price that will be favorable to the investor. Options allow investors to benefit from a particular direction of the market. You don't have to actually own the underlying asset to exercise an option on it. Owning options gives institutional investors, like insurance companies, a world of opportunity. Have you ever heard of renting with an option to buy? The option gives you the opportunity to live in the home for a year or so and pay rent but see which way the market goes before you commit to the purchase. Options give investors the same opportunity in the stock market.

- **Puts and Calls:** The two kinds of options are put and call. A put option is a contract giving the owner the right to sell a security at a certain price, by a certain time. By buying a put option on a security, you're betting that the security will go down before the specified date. A call option is just the opposite, allowing the buyer to buy a security at a specified price by a specified date. In this case, you're betting that the price of the security will go up, and if it does, you'll make money.

When you pay your premium to an insurance company for an IUL, the premium dollars go to cover various aspects of the contract to fulfill the promises made therein. A portion of the premium is deposited into the general fund, an investment-grade bond portfolio. Money in here goes to pay for the raw cost of the death benefit, called the cost of insurance. Then there are the administration fees and so forth. But after that is taken care of, the rest is used to purchase a call option. This is the "cream in the Twinkie," as they say. This call option allows the insurance company to follow the stock market by way of an index, such as the S&P, and pay the policy owner a reflective return on its upward movement (up to a cap) without having to actually be invested in the market.

This is a way of hedging against the risk of the market. If the index goes up, the insurance company simply calls the options. The returns (up to a cap) are then provided to the policy owner. If the market goes down, the insurance company allows the options to expire. No harm done.

Using Bond Portfolios

For the machinery of IUL to generate cash for its policy owners, it must involve the investment of the premium dollars but with ultimate safety.

The lion's share (approximately 95 percent) of this investment goes into predictable bond portfolios since corporate bonds, as far as safety is concerned, are the equivalent of cash. This is known as the general fund. That leaves 5 percent available for investment in call options on the market. If, for example, the IUL is mirroring the S&P 500 index and that index goes up, the insurance company can pass on those gains to policy owners. The bonds give the arrangement its safety net, and the call options provide the potential for growth when the index registers gains.

The main takeaway from all of this is that, when insurance companies make the promise that an IUL is a product that offers a guarantee of no losses and potential gains tied to the ups of the stock market, it is not smoke and mirrors. It is based on solid actuarial science and some brilliant (in my estimation) mathematical design.

Too Good to Be True? Not Really!

I'm like you. When something looks too good to be true, I usually start looking for the loopholes and the fine print. When IUL was first introduced, that's exactly what I did. I finally gave up when I had looked at all aspects of the investment looking for "gotchas" and couldn't find any. That's one of the reasons I have gone out of my way to explain every facet and feature of this product. We are all inclined to be skeptical of what we don't understand.

How would you have reacted if, without any explanation, I told you at the beginning of this book that I had found a retirement solution that would:

- pay your family a large sum of money, income tax-free, if you died;
- let you withdraw a tax-free retirement income;
- allow your account to grow with the ups of the market but never experience a market loss;
- let you access your money at any age;
- be immune to probate and lawsuits in most states; and
- make your contributions for you if you were disabled?

Well, would you have believed me? Or would you have called the men in white coats to take me away? I thought so.

But that just goes to show that sometimes something that is very good does come along and is just that, something very good and worth considering.

I advise people to never make financial decisions involving substantial sums of money and long-term commitments before making a thorough examination for themselves to determine the facts. The numbers with this product simply do not lie. Talk to a financial advisor who is knowledgeable about IUL and capable of answering all your questions to your complete satisfaction. Only then will you know if it is a fit for you.

PART II

Tax-Saving Strategies

The hardest thing in the world to understand is the income tax.
ALBERT EINSTEIN

CHAPTER 7

MAXIMIZING WEALTH BY MINIMIZING TAXES

T ax Freedom Day® is usually observed on a day in April and represents the day Americans in general have earned enough to pay their taxes. In 2017, Tax Freedom Day® fell on April 23rd, which meant, on average, Americans worked for Uncle Sam for almost the first four months before finally being able to pocket their paychecks.

In case you are wondering about the trademark sign, Florida businessman, Dallas Hostetler, conceived the idea of Tax Freedom Day® in 1948. Not only did Hostetler make it his business to calculate the date each year and announce it to the media, he trademarked the phrase. (I told you he was a businessman.) It does illustrate just how much we Americans pay in taxes.

Most people I know are decent, God-fearing, patriotic Americans who don't object to paying taxes. They appreciate having paved roads, good schools, and a country with well-defended borders. They know that paying taxes goes along with being a good citizen. They are perfectly willing to pay their fair share.

What they object to is paying more than their fair share. They want to contribute what they owe and not one penny more. What I have seen after working for decades with people in the area of financial planning is that most individuals do pay more than necessary in taxes. On the one hand, they work and save hard and invest diligently to accumulate wealth for their family's security, only to see much of it evaporate like the morning fog in unnecessary taxes.

Guess who is our best friend when it comes to helping us avoid unecessary taxation? The government! The IRS! There are perfectly legal and purely ethical ways to lessen your tax burden, and it's all right there in the IRS code. But if you expect to find these tax-saving measures by searching through the IRS code for phrases like "tax breaks" or "loopholes," you will be disappointed. Although you have the full blessings and approval of the IRS to implement these strategies, the IRS will never volunteer the information.

Have you ever heard of anyone getting a call from the IRS informing them of a tax deduction, exemption, or credit he or she failed to claim? Discovering these provisions is up to us. If a penny saved amounts to a penny earned, as Ben Franklin said, then every dollar we save in unnecessary taxes is one more dollar that can further our retirement goals.

As with anything engineered and administered by the federal government, our tax system is complex and ever-changing. There are twice as many words in the IRS code as there are in Leo Tolstoy's *War and Peace*, 1.3 million to be exact. The basic objective of tax planning is to enhance our personal wealth through tax reduction. When you stop and think about it, there are only three ways you can reduce taxes: reduce your income, increase your deductions, and/or take advantage of tax credits.

Reducing Income

The number-one way to reduce taxes is to reduce reportable income. (That's right. Not all income is reportable to the IRS.) For instance, when you contribute money to a qualified retirement plan, such as a 401(k) or a 403(b), the taxes are deferred, and as far as the government is concerned, those dollars were not earned. Don't worry. They will get their taxes out of you years later when you withdraw it during your retirement, but for the time being, you have dodged the taxman if you contribute to such a plan.

If you are self-employed and have an IRA or SEP program, you reduce your reportable income by the amount you contribute. If a penny saved is a penny earned, reducing the amount of adjusted gross income (AGI) on your tax return in effect increases your earnings since you keep the money working for you by earning interest instead of giving it to Uncle Sam.

Another way to reduce your AGI is through those wonderful things known as deductions. You can check with your tax advisor, but the last time I looked, page one on the 1040 form lists a bunch of deductions that you can take without going through the hassle of filling out Schedule A. The IRS refers to them as "adjustments" instead of "deductions," but what drops out the bottom is a reduced tax bill.

Exemptions and Business Expenses

Practically every taxpayer is able to take a standard deduction without having to itemize. It's a straight dollar amount you are able to deduct from your reportable income. Why? Just because. In 2017, the standard deduction for a single taxpayer was $6,350 and double that, $12,700, for married couples filing jointly.

Then there are itemized deductions. The way the IRS looks at it, if you own a hot dog stand and earn $50,000 but it costs you $10,000 to operate your business, you can itemize those expenses and deduct them from your income. What's left after you claim your deductions will be your AGI. But if your employment situation is simpler, that is, you work for a company earning $50,000 per year and you had no specific expenses, you may still claim the standard deduction as mentioned above.

Taxpayers can claim a personal exemption for themselves and any dependents they support. The personal exemption acts just like a tax deduction: it reduces your taxable income, so you end up paying taxes on less income.

This is only an overview. See your tax professional for all the details, or obtain and read the IRS code. But it should help illustrate that your tax bill is a little like the sticker price on a new automobile. The way the IRS rules are laid out, your tax bracket is this. You owe this much. But there are all kinds of ways to lower the amount you actually owe the IRS if you know where to find them. The more informed you are, the better you will be at avoiding unnecessary taxation.

Tax credits reduce your tax. In addition to the tax credits you get for saving money in qualified retirement plans, there are tax credits for taking college classes, adopting children, and several others.

While we are on the subject, all tax-qualified accounts come with rules, and if you don't play by them, you may wind up repaying taxes you thought you saved and paying penalties. For example, avoid early withdrawals from qualified retirement plans such as IRAs and 401(k) accounts if at all possible. The amount you withdraw will become part of your taxable income, and on top of that, there will be additional taxes to pay on early withdrawals (before age fifty-nine and a half). If you take a loan from your 401(k), make sure you pay it back, or you will owe additional taxes.

CHAPTER 8

TAX-FAVORED RETIREMENT STRATEGIES

Retirement is something you spend your entire life saving up for, and it should be a time that you are able to enjoy reduced income taxes now that you're not working. The retirement savings strategies you choose will play a large role in what tax rate you end up in during retirement. There are really three main ways to save for retirement:

- **Pre-Tax:** This very common strategy includes traditional IRAs, 401(k) accounts, and so forth. Money is deposited into the retirement account before any current taxes are taken out, and the money can grow over time. The theory here is that you have more money going into savings because you didn't have to pay tax on it and that amount is left to grow until you take it out. When you withdraw the money in retirement, the amount is taxable as income.
- **Tax-Deferred:** In this strategy, you set aside a portion of your after-tax income into a retirement account. The earnings in the account grow tax-deferred, meaning that, when you take out retirement income, taxes are due on the gain of the account and not the original investment. This type of account is commonly seen in an annuity or nondeductible IRA.

- **Tax-Free:** This is similar to the tax-deferred strategy. You contribute money to an account such as a Roth IRA on an after-tax basis, and when you withdraw money from that account in retirement, the principal and earnings are tax-free. It almost sounds too good to be true, doesn't it? Do you think that may be why the government imposes strict contribution limits on several of these types of accounts? Of course! Uncle Sam giveth, and Uncle Sam taketh away, but Uncle Sam is no fool. If you are to enjoy a tax-free strategy for building and withdrawing income in retirement, you will have to understand and thoroughly abide by the regulations placed on such a strategy by the federal government. That is one major secret of wealth-building, knowing where to look for the provisions of the IRS code.

Qualified Retirement Plans

Put simply, qualified retirement plans are all outlined in Section 401(a) of the tax code and can take on many different names: IRAs, 401(k) and 403(b) plans, SIMPLE IRA and SEP plans, defined benefit pension plans, 457 plans, and numerous others. Aside from Roth IRA plans, which we will discuss in more detail later, they are all some sort of plan where money is contributed into the specific account on a pre-tax basis and then is allowed to grow tax-free. When you take income out of the account (after age fifty-nine and a half), it is taxable to you at your ordinary income rate.

Traditional IRAs allow you to contribute on a pre-tax basis into the account, where they grow, tax-free, until you decide to start taking distributions after age fifty-nine and a half. Withdrawals made prior to age fifty-nine and a half will be subject to a 10 percent penalty. After age seventy and a half, you will be required to take what are called RMDs, a dictated yearly percentage of your account, which you must take out as income.

Table III				
(Uniform Lifetime)				
For Use by:				
Unmarried Owners				
Married Owners Whose Spouses Are Not More Than 10 Years Younger, and				
Married Owners Whose Spouses Are Not the Sole Beneficiaries of Their IRAs				
Age	Distribution Period	Age	Distribution Period
70	27.4	93	9.6
71	26.5	94	9.1
72	25.6	95	8.6
73	24.7	96	8.1
74	23.8	97	7.6
75	22.9	98	7.1
76	22	99	6.7
77	21.2	100	6.3
78	20.3	101	5.9
79	19.5	102	5.5
80	18.7	103	5.2
81	17.9	104	4.9
82	17.1	105	4.5
83	16.3	106	4.2
84	15.5	107	3.9
85	14.8	108	3.7
86	14.1	109	3.4
87	13.4	110	3.1
88	12.7	111	2.9
89	12	112	2.6
90	11.4	113	2.4
91	10.8	114	2.1
92	10.2	115 and over	1.9

Table obtained by IRS Publication 590-B [6]

6 (Source: IRS Publication 590-B (2015), Distributions from Individual Retirement Arrangements (IRAs))

401(k), 403(b), and 457 plans are all very similar to a traditional IRA but are sponsored by your employer or charitable organization. Employees and employers are able to contribute to these accounts. Your employer must set up these accounts, and they may offer some sort of matching to the dollars you contribute. The employer is able to receive a tax deduction for their matching contributions. The contribution limits to these types of accounts for 2017 is $18,000 and subject to additional cost of living increases.

Savings Incentive Match Plan for Employees (SIMPLE) and Simplified Employee Pension (SEP) IRAs are targeted toward self-employed individuals and those working for a small company. Again this is similar to a traditional IRA, but there are many rules regarding employer contributions and the amount the employer may claim as a tax deduction. An employee can contribute up to $12,500 into a SIMPLE IRA and up to $54,000 into a SEP IRA in 2017.

Defined benefit plans are more commonly referred to as pension plans. Instead of having a set contribution amount, you typically receive a fixed amount of retirement income, based upon your years of service to the company that offers the pension plan. The income you receive is taxable as income. As we've seen all across the news, these pension plans are becoming a thing of the past, as many states and municipalities have found these to be unsustainable.

The Roth IRA

Established by the Taxpayer Relief Act of 1997 (Public Law 105-34), the Roth IRA was named for its chief legislative sponsor, Senator William Roth of Delaware. The Roth IRA is an individual retirement account that offers no tax break in the accumulation phase but can provide a tax-free income in the distribution phase.

With the Roth, you have to follow the government's rules. You can withdraw your contributions (but not your earnings) any time with no taxes due and no penalties imposed. With the Roth, you must consider your tax rate. Will your tax rate be higher after you retire than it is now? Then a Roth makes better sense for you. As a savings vehicle, the Roth IRA matches up well with young workers whose incomes are lower. They probably won't miss the up-front tax deduction, but years from now, they will appreciate the tax-free income produced by decades of tax-free, compounded growth.

The primary appeal of the Roth is that they are tax-free on the back end. That also means they transfer to heirs tax-free. There is a limit on how much you can contribute ($5,500 per year in 2017) and how much you can earn ($196,000 in 2017 for Married Filers). You must also be a wage earner or have profits from a small business not in excess of the earnings limit. Like I said, there are lots of rules. Any program that offers tax breaks comes with pages of rules, it seems. But that is the job of your advisor to understand them and guide your footsteps through the minefield.

Keep in mind that the wide popularity of IRAs is rooted in their obvious tax benefits. I am beginning to see more and more people appreciate the advantages of tax-free income in retirement. Remember, the Roth IRA is not an investment in and of itself. You might look at it as a tax-advantaged wrapper for any number of things, including mutual funds, annuities, CDs, exchange-traded funds (ETFs), stocks, or bonds.

You can fund both traditional and Roth IRAs from your personal contributions, or you can use them as the destination for a rollover from a 401(k) or similar qualified retirement savings account. Many establish an IRA if they are self-employed or if their employer doesn't offer a retirement plan. Some open them if their employer offers a retirement plan but does not match contributions.

Roth IRAs have another favorable tax feature: you can withdraw your contributions at any time and for any reason without owning taxes or penalties. Only the earnings on those contributions are subject to taxes and penalties if you withdraw them before age fifty-nine and a half.

Roth IRA Conversions

You can open a Roth IRA, or if you have money in a traditional IRA or retirement plan with a former employer, you can move some or all of it into a Roth by completing a conversion. A word of caution: Roth conversions are not for everyone, and each situation is different. It is a good idea to seek professional assistance in making the decision to do a Roth conversion. Conversions from a traditional IRA to a Roth are subject to ordinary income taxes. Sometimes just reviewing the rules can make the decision for you.

For instance, if the rules don't allow you to deduct your traditional IRA contribution, then a Roth may be a better choice, assuming you're eligible. If you have the option of a deductible traditional IRA or a Roth IRA, the choice comes down to whether you prefer to pay taxes now or later. Do you think that income tax rates will be higher in the future, or do you anticipate that you will have more income in retirement and slide into a higher tax bracket?

Roth 401(k)

In January 2006, the IRS made it possible for employees to choose a Roth option on their 401(k) plans, and it seems to be gaining in popularity. The Roth 401(k) options make saving for retirement in the workplace more flexible, but there are now more rules than ever. Employees can elect to make after-tax contributions or the traditional, deferred pre-tax contributions. You pay taxes on earnings when you take them out of the traditional 401(k), but earnings are never taxable with the Roth 401(k).

As with the Roth IRA, the Roth 401(k) options seem to favor younger workers with lower incomes who think they will be paying higher taxes in retirement because they will have accumulated more taxable income. As I write this, many American workers aren't even aware that Roth 401(k) options exist. That's because many smaller employers don't offer them yet, but I think that is starting to change.

Tax-Free versus Tax-Deferred

Tax-deferred is good, but tax-free is better. Picture this. You are a farmer. It's planting time. You walk into your local farmer's co-op to buy seed for this year's crop. As you approach the counter to pay for your sacks of seed, a fellow dressed up like Uncle Sam, wearing a hat that says "IRS," comes up to you and makes you a proposition.

"I'll make you a deal," says Uncle Sam. "You can pay me taxes on that seed now and be done with it, or you can defer those taxes and pay me taxes on your harvest when it comes in. Which will it be?"

What would you do? Pay the tax on the seed, of course! But tax-deferred plans, like traditional IRAs and 401(k)s, have us paying taxes on the harvest. Millions of Americans just follow the herd and invest their retirement money into plans that save them a few dollars on the short run but cost them a bundle in the long run.

Also with a qualified plan, you are at a contribution disadvantage. Let's say you come by a sizable chunk of money, say $200,000, and you want to place it in your tax-qualified plan. You can't. Tax-qualified plans come with a contribution limit. Roth IRAs, which are taxed going in but tax-free coming out, come with contribution limits and other restrictions.

Let's say the individual with a high net worth has $500,000 he or she wishes to invest. What are the choices: a bank, credit union, CDs, stocks, bonds, or mutual funds? Every one of those options is taxable. With most, the interest you earn is counted as annual income and is reportable on your yearly tax return. At some point, you will pay taxes on the gains.

Is there anywhere you can invest $500,000 or $1 million where there are tax advantages, safety, and excellent growth potential? I sometimes ask that question to a group, and I can almost see the wheels turning in their minds of folks in the audience as they attempt to reconcile these three criteria: tax-advantages, safety, and excellent growth potential.

Most people, even experienced investors, come up blank. One choice will have good growth potential but will come with market risk. Another will be risk-free but with little growth potential. Likewise with tax advantages.

I keep my eyes peeled and my ear pretty close to the ground when it comes to developments in the financial world, and I cannot think of any other investment that includes all of these criteria. I'm sorry if it sounds like I am tooting this horn repeatedly, but once you fully grasp the way IUL works, you wonder why more people in the financial community aren't aware of it!

Life Insurance Retirement Plans

Can you purchase an IUL policy and pay for it in regular monthly premiums? Of course you can. People do it every day. But the way to really squeeze the best performance out of this high-powered financial instrument is to fund it up front with a lump sum of cash. Why? Overfunding an IUL transforms a life insurance policy into a cash-generating investment vehicle with amazing possibilities.

Not everyone will be in a position to do this, I realize. This tax-advantaged wealth-building strategy is not a good fit for everyone who reads this book. I know that too. But I would be remiss in my responsibilities as a financial counselor if I didn't point an opportunity to build significant wealth and generate tax-free income. Businesspeople and high net worth investors are usually perfect candidates for this strategy. Why? They have the resources to supercharge the cash value portion of the policy.

Individuals who come into large sums of money, either through an inheritance or from the sale of a piece of property or business, have a good problem on their hands. They have to invest the money somewhere. And there are only so many places to put money. And most of them involve trade-offs in one way or another. Stocks, bonds, and mutual funds, for example, offer high growth potential but come with risk. CDs at the bank are very safe but offer little growth potential.

What about traditional IRAs and qualified plans that offer tax-free growth but are taxable at distribution? They're okay, but in my opinion, compared with the tax-free growth and the potential for a tax-free income stream offered by investment-grade life insurance, it is a no-brainer. IUL mirrors the benefits of Roth IRAs but does not have the rules and regulations that limit how much you can invest.

Flexibility of Premium

As we were examining how IUL would fit into one couple's financial plan, I explained to them that Congress has placed a limit on the amount of money that can be placed into an IUL policy. That was when the wife asked what I thought was a brilliant question, "Why would the government care how much insurance you buy?"

You can see why she would ask such a question. After all, the IRS does not care how much you invest in the stock market. Nor do they mind if you place billions in a bank account. So why would Congress mind if you loaded up on as much cash value life insurance as you could afford?

The answer, of course, lies in the fact that IUL is one of the few legal tax shelters left. That's why TAMRA declared a maximum amount of tax-advantaged life insurance an individual could buy.

"I get it," the husband said after I explained this. "If the IRS puts a limit on how much of something you can own, it must be a pretty good thing to own."

I think he got the point. What we essentially have is a situation where the insurance company sets the minimum amount of premium required and the IRS sets the maximum amount of premium allowed. Flexible premium allows the savvy investor to adjust premiums within that range to maximize tax-advantaged cash growth. The minimum premium is the raw cost of the death benefit. Anything in excess of that goes straight to the cash value portion of the policy.

Take, for example, a hypothetical case where a thirty-five-year-old male who earns $150,000 per year purchases a $1 million IUL policy. What would be the minimum premium required by the insurance company for such a policy? I will guess and say around $300 per month. But that is not the maximum premium TAMRA allows to pay into the policy. Let's say that our policy owner owns a business that is doing quite well and he is able to put a hefty lump sum into the policy per year. Would it be to his advantage to do so? Absolutely!

For one thing, he is able to become his own bank. Let's say he could pay $35,000 per year into the policy, in addition to the minimum premium. That would likely boost his cash value considerably. And let's say he needs a business loan ten years down the road to expand. He can always borrow from the bank and pay the going interest rate. But what if he could borrow against his own cash value at a low rate of interest and, in essence, pay himself back? Wouldn't that be a smart thing to do?

The IRS limits how much you can pump into an IUL each year before it loses its tax-advantaged status and becomes what is called a modified endowment contract (MEC). Not to worry. The insurance company will let the policy owner know exactly where that line is to make sure he doesn't cross it.

Does the young man have to commit to a certain amount of premium over and above the $300 per month? No. It may be that he cannot afford to overfund the contract at first. Maybe he is just getting started.

Or what if he could set aside $5,000 one year and $10,000 the next? No problem. That's what flexible premium is all about.

The Carryover Provision

As we have already mentioned, the federal government says you can only put so much per year into an IUL contract before it becomes a MEC and a taxable investment. Let's say the maximum amount allowable under TAMRA for our young businessman to contribute is $40,000 per year. If he puts in only $10,000 one year (leaving $30,000 on the table, so to speak), can he put $70,000 into his policy the next year? Yes! Thanks, Uncle Sam.

What if he only puts in $10,000 per year for twenty years and then inherits a large sum of money? Can he sink that into his policy if he wants to? Yes! It's called "carryover," and it particularly favors a business owner who wishes to use an IUL as a retirement vehicle when he sells his business.

From the informal surveys I have taken, most business owners intend to sell their businesses when they retire. What happens when you come into a large sum of money from such a transaction? If you just got a mental picture of Uncle Sam with his hand out, stuffing his pockets with the proceeds of what you have worked all of your life to build up, you are right on.

Did the light bulb just go off as to why IUL can be a tremendous advantage to a business owner who will at some time in the future sell his enterprise and have a lump sum of money he or she now has to invest somewhere? That entrepreneur will not be thinking about the return on the money as much as the return of the money. The word "taxes" will be flashing on and off like a big neon sign. An IUL he bought years ago will be the perfect legal tax haven for such a lump sum.

Let that sink in, tax-deferred growth and tax-free access plus the ability to pass on that wealth to heirs income tax-free. I have scoured the financial product landscape, and I cannot find any other product out there where such tax-advantaged benefits exist. If you, dear reader, know of any, I would appreciate you contacting me at your earliest convenience using the information supplied on the back cover of this book. I will put it under my electron microscope and check it out!

Proper Planning Is Essential

One thing I have tried to do in the pages of this book is acquaint you with the ins and outs, the pros and cons, and as many details about IUL that I feel are essential for you to have a clear understanding of what it is, what it does, and how it does it. Because it has a few moving parts, IUL needs to be properly structured if you are to get the full benefit of its provisions.

Unlike traditional IRAs, Roth IRAs, and qualified plans, IULs have no contribution limits, but they must comply with TEFRA/DEFRA regulations in order to maintain their tax-advantaged status. They are especially appropriate investments for affluent investors, small business owners, or entrepreneurs who may not have a qualified pension plan in place. Or maybe they just want to accumulate more than qualified plans permit.

The tax-free liquidity of IULs can give the policyholder the option of buying property, making improvements, or purchasing expensive equipment or assets while keeping unlimited access to the principal within the policy.

CHAPTER 9

HOW CAN THE INCOME BE TAX-FREE?

J ust the mention of the phrase "tax-free income" is music to the ears. But the first thing that comes to mind when you hear the word "free" these days is, "What's the catch?" I owe it to my clients to look at every investment vehicle that comes across my desk with an electron microscope. As I mentioned earlier, I have looked at IUL from every angle, trying to find a "gotcha," and I simply couldn't find one. Granted, there are a few moving parts but no negative surprises. So how can the income be tax-free?

First, remember that the IRS gives a life insurance policy a unique status, one that few other financial instruments are provided, in that the proceeds from a life insurance policy death benefit are income tax-free. A life insurance policy is a tax-deferred financial instrument, but it is not necessarily a tax-free financial instrument. The cash value within an IUL policy grows tax-free. If you simply withdraw it, you create a taxable event. You will owe both capital gains and income taxes. Not good!

But what if you could find another way to access your policy's cash value without making outright withdrawals? Well, you can do exactly that through policy loan provisions. At this point, some who are unacquainted with the way the gears of an insurance contract work will scratch their heads and make a face. Loans? I don't want to borrow money!

But we are speaking a different language here. Don't let the word "loan" scare you. This is a unique provision of the IUL contract. Once you grasp it, you will smile and give a low whistle of admiration for the creative genius of the product design people at the insurance companies who developed this facet of IUL.

Remember that loans are not taxed. If you borrow the money to buy something, what you bought may be taxed, but you don't pay taxes on the loan, do you? Take a car loan, for example. You pay taxes on the car, but not on the bank loan. The car serves as the collateral for the loan. In the same manner, you can use the cash value within an insurance contract as collateral and access that cash (without actually withdrawing it) by taking advantage of the policy loan provisions, thereby avoiding taxation. Here's how the procedure works:

If you are the policy owner, can you withdraw the amount you have paid in premiums into the policy tax-free? Of course you can. You paid taxes on that money going in, didn't you? So you can access that cash in the form of a withdrawal (subject to the surrender charges if they apply) tax-free. If you make a withdrawal of an amount over and above the money you put into the policy, it will be taxed as ordinary income. Why? You are withdrawing money on which taxes have not been paid.

But here's the sweet part. With life insurance, you can borrow or take out a loan against your cash value, using your cash value as collateral. Is the money coming out of your cash value? No, it is simply the proceeds of a loan against your cash value.

"But wait a minute!" you may say. "I don't want to have to incur interest charges on a loan and be stuck with indebtedness in retirement."

But what if you were able to borrow the money at zero interest? And what if you didn't have to pay back the loan during your lifetime? That's a completely different story, isn't it?

No, we are not merely dealing with semantics. It may be a finely drawn line, but there is a clear distinction between withdrawing your cash value outright and taking out a policy loan using your cash value as collateral, both in the eyes of the IRS and in the rules spelled out in the insurance contract.

A question I like to ask when I am called on to speak on the subject of taxes is, "Who do you think pays more in unnecessary taxes? The informed or the uninformed?" The answer is obvious, the uninformed. We are merely taking advantage of provisions that have been there all along in the tax code and using the stipulations put forth in the insurance contract.

"But how can they call it a loan if they charge zero interest?"

That's a good question. It is best explained this way. With policy loans, you do get charged an interest rate, but the insurance company essentially removes an amount equivalent to the interest charges from the cash value, which is collateral for the loan. So let's say the interest rate on the policy loan is 5 percent. If the insurance company on the one hand charges you 5 percent but, on the other, pays you 5 percent on the cash value that stands as collateral for the loan, how much interest are you actually paying? Zero.

The word in the industry for this is "wash loan." With 5 percent in and 5 percent out, it's a wash. But by redirecting the flow of the money in such a way, you have met the qualifications for accessing money from the cash value of your policy without causing a taxable event.

If you are one of those people who is satisfied with "six thirty-two" when you ask what the time is, you can skip this paragraph. But if you want to take the back of the watch off and see the gears tick, here are some finer details.

When you take money from your cash value, whether it's in the form of a withdrawal or a loan, you are reducing the cash value for certain and maybe the death benefit as well. You don't want to do anything to cause the policy to lapse, and that can happen if you take out too much money too early. That's why it is best to follow the guidelines in the policy and allow a qualified agent who is fully trained in how these vehicles work to walk you through the process.

Insurance companies provide software with these investment-grade policies that will give you accurate information on how much money you should access in the way of a withdrawal and how much you should access in the way of a policy loan. Each company has different provisions and requirements. If you intend to use IUL as a vehicle to generate a tax-free retirement, you will likely be overfunding the policy to take full advantage of the tax-free provisions.

As previously discussed, there is a limit as to how much money you can contribute to your policy and keep it within this tax-advantaged window. Your advisor can guide you through this area as well. It is best to look at these vehicles long term and wait ten years or so before you take policy loans.

Tax-Free Cash Income

Through the policy loan provision of your IUL policy, you can access amounts equal to your cash value during your lifetime. Because the money comes to you in the form of a loan, it is not recorded as income on your tax return and, therefore, is not taxed by the IRS. Are you able to use the money any way you wish? Absolutely! That's the beauty of it. That's what makes the strategy work. You are working within the framework of a life insurance policy and its unique tax status.

When people create retirement incomes through ordinary stock market investment accounts, not only are they subject to the unpredictability and volatility of the market, the funds they drain from their account are fully taxable as ordinary income. With IRAs, SEPs, 401(k)s, and other tax-qualified accounts, the money grows tax-deferred but is fully taxed when withdrawn. Roth IRAs are the only retirement savings vehicles that can provide tax-free income, which is why some refer to the income-generating capability of IULs as a "giant Roth," only without the strict contribution limits.

Using Insurance Trusts

Life insurance death benefits are income tax-free but not necessarily estate tax-free. This is where irrevocable life insurance trusts (ILITs) come in. The way the IRS looks at life insurance policies, if you are the policy owner, that is, you have the right to name beneficiaries and so forth, the policy is included in your estate and subject to estate taxes upon your death. But it is possible to make sure your heirs get the proceeds of the death benefit without having to include them in your estate. How? By changing the owner of the policy from you as an individual to an ILIT. That way, when you pass away, your tax-free loans are paid off with the income tax-free death benefit. Whatever is left over goes to your heirs' income and estate tax-free.

Once you create an ILIT, you will likely designate an individual whom you trust, such as a spouse or a sibling, as your trustee. For example, your

ILIT can provide that your surviving spouse will benefit from the proceeds during his or her life, and upon his or her death, the remaining proceeds will be distributed to your children. A word of caution regarding this: the IRS requires you make these arrangements three years prior to your death if you are not the original policy owner.

Not for Everybody

If you are sitting there reading this and wondering why IULs are not on the evening news as the best thing in the financial world since the invention of paper money, it's probably because, as financial vehicles, they are a bit complex. They don't fit easily into a sound bite and bear some explaining, which this book attempts to do.

Also, they are not for everyone. Keep in mind, you may intend to build a tax-free retirement, but you are also buying life insurance. You must be healthy enough to qualify. Also the strategy works better for those who are high income earners. It is not a short-term strategy either. The key factor in all of this—the pivotal point that makes the strategy work—is the income tax-free death benefit. The policy must remain in force until the death of the insured. If the policy is allowed to lapse or is canceled, you have just created a taxable event. Not good!

That's why you need to have your agent run an illustration that extends all the way to at least age 120 for the insured. Illustrations to age ninety or ninety-five are too risky. The income stream that the illustration produces may be more conservative, but it's best to be on the safe side.

There are other factors to consider as well, such as the rating of the insurance company from which you purchase an IUL. I suggest you use a financial planner who is fully conversant and thoroughly knowledgeable on how IUL insurance works and can answer all of your questions…and even some that you may not think to ask!

PART III

Estate Planning

"In this world, nothing can be said to be certain, except death and taxes."
BENJAMIN FRANKLIN

CHAPTER 10

THE PROBLEM WITH PROBATE

You can't have a discussion about estate planning without talking about the evils of probate. The word "probate" comes from the Latin word "probatum," which connotes providing proof of something, in this case, a will or the settling of an estate. Probate is the legal process by which our worldly goods and possessions are distributed to others after we die. In an estate of some size, it becomes legally necessary to prove the will in a court of law before all who may have an interest in what we leave to whom when we leave this world behind. So why is it a problem?

First, it can be a costly and time-consuming procedure. If the estate is of any size, the probate process will likely involve probate attorneys, a judge, and the services of an appraiser and an accountant, plus fees and court costs. Some estates are complicated. State laws vary, and if the deceased owned property in other states, the heirs may face multiple probate sessions to get it all straightened out. You would think that there would be some kind of standard price structure for the services associated with probate, but there is not. Fees and charges vary from one legal community to another and from state to state.

I have seen long delays between the filing of the will and the distribution of funds and property. One woman told me that her husband had passed away six years ago and his estate was still in probate. I asked her why, and she said his relatives were squabbling over the money. Those kinds of disputes are settled at the expense of the estate, and tales of that kind are not rare.

Assets of an estate are frozen during the probate process so accountants and appraisers can do an inventory and assess the value of the estate. This takes time and costs money. Also the probate process is a public record, which means that anyone and everyone can see what you put in your will and can view, print, and publish details about what you owned and whom you owed. Loss of privacy and embarrassment aside, the biggest danger in the probate process is a magnet for unscrupulous people coming out of the woodwork to prey on heirs once they learn of a large inheritance. By its public nature, the probate process also invites contest. Individuals are allowed take issue with the provisions of a will, and creditors can make claims against the estate.

Probate Horror Stories

Stories abound about famous people who left behind estate messes because they failed to plan properly. Famous people may make the accounts more memorable, but ordinary folks in mainstream America make the same planning mistakes every day. We just never hear about them.

- **Anna Nicole Smith:** You remember Anna Nicole Smith, the former Playboy Playmate, exotic dancer, and reality TV star? Her real name was Vickie Lynn Marshall, and her case has to be among the most bizarre. She married Texas oil billionaire, J. Howard Marshall, when he was eighty-nine years old. As I write this, the case has been ongoing for nearly two decades with no end in sight and millions of dollars spent in litigation. Let's see if I can explain this complicated estate train wreck. Smith married Marshall in 1994. Fourteen months later, Marshall died and left her out of the will. He left everything to Pierce Marshall, one of his sons. The probate proceedings started soon afterward with Smith claiming what she considered to be her rightful share of the $1.6 billion estate. Pierce Marshall died in June 2006 at age sixty-seven with the case still unsettled. The case started in Louisiana and then moved to Texas and finally California. A California judge awarded Smith $475 million, but she never saw the money because she died in 2007 from a drug overdose. The case seems to have a life of its own with unceasing appeals, reversals, reappeals, claims, and counterclaims. Even if the Smith estate wins its latest appeal, observers of the bizarre legal battle say legal fees will be so much that Smith's young daughter, Dannielynn Birkhead, may never see a dollar of the fortune.

- **Marilyn Monroe:** The 1950s pinup of legend, Marilyn Monroe, is also a poster girl for how not to plan an estate. She died August 5, 1962, and her estate is making more money than the blond bombshell ever made while she was alive. The peculiar thing is where the money goes. The image of Marilyn is everywhere: magazines, books, T-shirts, and coffee mugs. Every time it is reproduced, hefty royalties are generated and paid, only not to anyone related to Marilyn. In her will, she left most of her estate to Lee Strasberg, her acting coach. Strasberg died in 1982, and his second wife, who had no connection to Marilyn whatsoever, inherited his estate. She, in turn, hired a firm that specializes in managing the estates of dead celebrities to license Monroe's image. The management firm keeps Marilyn alive, so to speak, by capitalizing on her legend while Strasberg's widow cashes the checks.

- **Phillip Seymour Hoffman:** When forty-six-year-old actor Phillip Seymour Hoffman died suddenly in 2014, he was wealthy and famous. His estate was valued at approximately $35 million. He had apparently filed a will in 2004 after the birth of his first child, but he never updated the document to include two other children he had with his partner, Marianne O'Donnell. The decision (or non-decision) not to marry was, of course, a personal one, but had they married, it would have prevented about $12 million from going to the IRS. Federal law in 2014 offered an estate tax exemption for the first $5.32 million, but anything exceeding that is taxed up to 40 percent. New York State gets another 16 percent. Total taxes due from the Hoffman estate came to just over $15 million. Had he married O'Donnell, she would have qualified for an unlimited marital deduction. Because two of Hoffman's children were not named in the will, it remained unclear at the time of this writing how they would be cared for and by whom. It is a reminder of how prudent it is to update life documents following each life event, such as a death, birth, divorce, or marriage.

- **James Dean:** James Dean, who died in an automobile accident at age twenty-four in 1955, left no will. His entire estate, including millions in royalty and licensing income, passed to his father, who had reportedly abandoned him as a child.

- **John Denver:** The singer who died in 1997 in a plane crash had no estate plan, and it took six years to settle his $19 million estate. His children had to pay tens of millions of dollars in unnecessary taxes.

- **James Gandolfini:** The actor who played mob boss Tony Soprano on the HBO series, *The Sopranos*, died of a heart attack in 2013, leaving behind a net worth of around $70 million. He had made a will and created at least one trust. But *New York Daily News* would later report that federal estate taxes would eat up more than $20 million of the estate and New York estate taxes would consume another $10 million or so. The problem was that Gandolfini left less than 20 percent of his estate to his wife, who would have enjoyed an estate tax exemption. Readers of the *Daily News* were left scratching their heads, wondering why he didn't want his wife to receive the bulk of his estate. (See how public these things get?) Most of his estate went to other family members and a former assistant. Surely someone of his wealth could have afforded an estate plan that would have employed various trusts to shelter the vast majority of his estate from the taxman and keep the details of his private life out of the public eye.

- **Prince:** The most recent example of failing to plan your estate is the famed musician who passed away suddenly in 2016 without even a basic will. While the true value of his estate is unknown, best estimates are currently estimating about $300 Million, of which the greatest windfall will go to the government. To make matters worse and highlight the need for estate liquidity, it is being said that his libraries of unreleased music may have to be sold in order to cover the estate tax liability. Prince may be some of the best proof we have that it is never too young to meet with a professional and carefully draft an estate plan.

We have only scratched the surface of these examples. These people, like others who neglect this important area of their financial lives, didn't plan to fail. They failed to plan.

Planning Avoids Probate Problems

Proper estate planning can reduce or eliminate nearly all of the evils of probate. The psychological benefits of planning your estate are obvious. Heirs can grieve in private without worrying about court proceedings. They aren't forced to watch the value of the estate erode in the probate process. It is news to some that strategies exist that can allow the bulk of your estate to bypass the probate process. Some of these strategies include:

- **Trusts:** Just to make the point with clients, I sometimes like to tell them that one sure way to avoid probate is to get rid of their property. That usually gets their attention. Then I quickly explain that it's not what they are thinking. The idea behind a trust is essentially to rename your property so it is legally not yours but belongs to an entity. The laws allow you to control the entity, however. This, in turn, allows you to maintain control of the assets. With some trusts, you can be the trust's beneficiary. For example, a revocable living trust is a written agreement that covers three phases of your life: while you are alive and healthy, if you should become incapacitated, and after your death. Simply having a revocable living trust is not enough by itself to avoid probate. You must fund the trust. To be probate-proof, the trust must own your assets. A properly prepared trust trumps a will and its provisions in the eyes of the court. Any competent estate attorney will know how to properly prepare the trust to comply with state laws that apply and thereby protect your estate where it is vulnerable.

- **Beneficiaries:** I find that many are not aware of just how important the beneficiary line is on important financial documents. Most folks associate the word "beneficiary" with life insurance policies. But annuities, IRAs, retirement savings accounts, and other financial documents contain a provision to name one or more beneficiaries. Did you know that, in most cases, these designated beneficiaries are uncontestable and cannot be affected by probate? One of the first things I do for clients is a document assessment. Then I review the beneficiary line. I have seen some documents where the beneficiary of hundreds of thousands of dollars in assets is an ex-spouse. Can you imagine how that would play out if the individual remarries and effectively disinherits his or her spouse by neglecting to update important investment documents? In some cases, the designated beneficiary line has been left blank or filled in with the word "estate." If a will specifies that all your assets will go to your spouse when you die and yet a life insurance policy or an annuity specifies that a former spouse is the beneficiary, where do you think the money will go? Right. To the former spouse. Beneficiary designations take precedence over the provisions of a will and are not subject to the evils of probate. I apologize if I appear to be repeating myself on this issue or maybe hammering the nail when it is already in the plank, but I cannot tell you how many times I have seen such simple things derail estates. I recommend you have a primary beneficiary and a contingent beneficiary on these documents. Usually, with a married couple, the surviving spouse will be the primary beneficiary, and the children will be secondary beneficiaries. Make sure you designate the beneficiary by name, not by the designation "spouse," "husband," or "wife." Please don't put the word "estate," anticipating the provisions of your will would cover it. A competent estate planner would never allow that one to slide by unnoticed. If there is not enough room on the line to articulate your wishes, add as many sheets of paper to the document as needed to explicitly articulate your requests. What happens if, God forbid, you and your spouse are both killed in an automobile accident? Is it clear to any who are left behind where the proceeds of the account are to go and how? Some account custodians require a change of beneficiary form to update documents. These can usually be downloaded and printed out in a matter of minutes. Keep in mind that, if the beneficiary is a minor, an adult needs to be designated as the administrator of the funds. This will usually be the guardian named in your will but does not have to be. You can also create a trust and name a trustee. The point is, insurance companies and other large financial institutions don't write checks to kids.

- **Joint Ownership with Rights of Survivorship:** Joint ownership is one way to make it clear who gets what in an estate. Obviously, if a person's name is on the document as co-owner, that individual continues to own the asset when the other co-owner dies. It's the same as with a joint bank account. There is no probate wrangling about who owns the money in a joint bank account when one of the owners dies, is there? It is the same with an investment account or real estate property. Often it must be articulated on the document that the account, property, or asset is owned by joint tenants with rights of survivorship, not as tenants in common. (See your estate attorney on this. State laws vary.)

A Caution on Joint Ownership

Sometimes we encounter clients who have attempted estate planning by putting accounts into joint ownership with their children. While this may ensure that the asset in question goes to the child upon their death, it would forego the step-up in cost basis that is granted to those who inherit accounts. Additional complications may arise if the child predeceases you, or if either of you become the subject of a creditor claim.

CHAPTER 11

WILLS AND LIVING TRUSTS

As I said before, the easiest way to avoid the probate of your estate is simply to get rid of all of your property. If you own no property, there is nothing to probate, is there? That's essentially what a trust does. In essence, you give away your assets to an entity over which you still maintain control and of which you are beneficiary. Trusts fall into four distinct classifications:

- **Revocable:** This is where you can undo, or revoke, the trust at any time since you are the grantor (a legal term).
- **Irrevocable:** Once this type of trust is established, it cannot be undone.
- *Inter Vivos*: This Latin phrase means "between the living," and it refers to a transfer or a gift made during one's lifetime. So an *inter vivos* trust is in effect while you are still alive.
- **Testamentary:** This kind of trust takes effect during your lifetime and is usually created in wills or other documents ordered by their wording to take effect when you die. By their very nature, all testamentary trusts are irrevocable.

Pros and Cons of Revocable Trusts

Living trusts do a good job of avoiding probate, and they allow you to get past the pesky pitfalls of joint tenancy, but you need to know something about living trusts. They offer no asset protection whatsoever! Why? Because they are revocable!

The grantor of a living trust has the authority to undo the trust at any point during his or her lifetime. It is the same as changing a will. All it takes is a few strokes of the pen. Revocability may be good in some respects, but it renders the trust useless when it comes to protecting your assets. Revocable trusts are vulnerable trusts.

Let's say that, after your death, your creditors want to seize the assets owned by a revocable living trust. All they have to do is ask the court to step into the shoes, as it were, of the grantor and revoke the trust. The trust shield has just been compromised, and it is as if you own the assets personally once more. With that change in ownership status, they are now vulnerable to the probate process.

That is not to say that living trusts are valueless. I believe they are a crucial part of any estate plan. If you place ownership within living trusts instead of in your personal name, you stand to save much in the way of taxes and probate fees down the road. But if asset protection is what you are aiming for, then you need to establish an irrevocable trust. Do you give up control with an irrevocable trust? Absolutely. But that is the price you pay—and some think it is well worth it—to have the maximum in asset protection. This course makes a lot of sense when the assets will ultimately go to your beneficiaries anyway and you do not need them in liquid form for your own financial security.

Successor Trustees

When you die, who takes over a living trust? That is up to you. While you are still alive, as the trustee of your living trust, you will name someone or an entity, if that is applicable, as the successor trustee. That individual will collect income due your estate, pay off remaining debts and taxes, and make sure assets are distributed according to your wishes. This individual or entity acts much like the executor of a will, only their actions are not subject to probate and interference by the courts. A successor trustee is a fiduciary. As such, he or she is required by law to follow the instructions of the trust and act strictly according to its provisions.

CHAPTER 12

ESTATE TAXES: A MOVING TARGET

How are estate tax laws like the weather? Both constantly changing, and are difficult to forecast. I know of one man who planned carefully in order to reduce the big bite that he anticipated the government would take out of his considerable estate. As things turned out, he died in July 2010 when there was no estate tax. If he had died a few months earlier or later, however, his heirs would have had to pay millions of dollars. (His estate was valued at well over a billion dollars.) When the Bush tax cuts (officially the Economic Growth and Tax Reconciliation Act of 2001) were put into place in 2002, they had an expiration date of 2011, but the American Taxpayer Relief Act of 2012 extended them. The US Congress passed legislation on January 1, 2013 that made the estate tax permanent at $5 million, the same as it had been in 2002, with the provision that it would be adjusted for inflation every year.

As I write this, the federal gift/estate tax exemption stands at $5.49 million (2017) per person. That means that every person may leave, give away, or bequeath up to $5.49 million without owing any estate tax. That also means that the federal estate tax will only affect America's wealthiest families.

It is common knowledge that the federal estate tax exists, but it comes as a surprise to some people that states impose an additional state estate tax. As of this writing, the Illinois estate tax exemption is $4 million. Unlike the federal estate tax, it is not adjusted for inflation, is not scheduled to increase, and is not portable between spouses. A word of caution: state estate laws are subject to change. If you own real estate in other states or have a beneficiary that lives in another state, those laws will influence your estate.

Since the beginning of the twenty-first century, planning for the estate tax has been like aiming at a moving target. Perhaps it will return to stability, but nothing is for sure. Look at how dramatically the federal estate tax has changed in recent history. It was $1 million in 2002, $2 million in 2006, unlimited in 2010, $5 million in 2011, and $5.49 million as this book is being written in 2017. From a planning perspective, it is prudent to hope for the best but have an estate plan in place to address the likeliest scenario.

Portability for Spouses

What exactly is spousal portability? It is a popular feature of recent estate tax law that allows spouses to combine their estate tax exemptions. It lets married couples leave (or give away) nearly $11 million (in 2017) to heirs without owing taxes.

In the beginning of 2013, portability became a permanent part of the estate tax laws. If the first spouse to pass away fails to use up his or her individual gift/tax estate tax exemption, the surviving spouse can use what's left. That essentially doubles the individual exemption amount for couples. As an example, if each member of a couple has $4 million in assets and the first one to die leaves everything to the other spouse, then no estate tax is owed. Why? Property left to the surviving spouse is tax-free. What happens when the surviving spouse later dies and leaves $8 million to their children ($4 million plus the $4 million inherited from the other spouse)? No estate tax will be due. This is the case even when the estate is over the exemption amount because the estate can use some of the unused exemption from the first spouse.

That's portability. To take advantage of this estate tax provision, an estate tax return must be filed when the first spouse dies even if no tax is due. These are complex returns, and you need to consult a tax professional who is familiar with gift and estate tax law. A federal tax known as a "generation skipping transfer tax" is levied on large transfers of wealth that skip a generation, a gift from a grandparent to a grandchild, for example.

CHAPTER 13

STRATEGIES TO AVOID THE ESTATE TAX

According to the popular idiom, nothing in life is certain except death and taxes. "When it's your time to go, it's your time to go" is the mantra of fatalists everywhere. When someone dies unexpectedly in a freak accident, you will hear people say, "I guess his number was up."

I can't comment on the inevitability of the Grim Reaper. I will leave that to the philosophers and men and women of the cloth. What I can tell you is that, while not all taxes can be avoided, the estate tax is one that can be circumvented in many cases or at least minimized through proper planning. But since it is one of the most complex of all the tax laws in the land, sidestepping it requires careful planning.

Some Americans view the estate tax as unfair. After all, they reason, the money in question has already been taxed. Proponents of the estate tax think differently. They contend that it is a fair way of leveling the playing field when it comes to wealth in America. From a planning point of view, I recommend you collect as much information on taxes as possible. Who do you think pays more in taxes? The informed or the uninformed? You're right. The uninformed! It is also important to keep up-to-date. To say that tax laws are subject to change is an understatement. Here are some things you need to know about estate taxes:

- **Exemptions:** As we have already pointed out, federal estate tax only applies if your taxable estate exceeds a certain level, $5.49 million in 2017. The United States has a unified gift and estate tax system. That means that taxable gifts count against your estate tax exemption. If you make taxable gifts during your lifetime, you will essentially use up some of that $5.49 million in advance. The trade-off is that you didn't have to pay gift tax when you made the gift.

- **Gift Tax Exclusions:** These continue to change. As of 2017, you could make a cash or property gift valued at up to $14,000 without incurring a gift tax. Not all gifts or bequests are subject to tax. The marital deduction allows you to give as much to a spouse as you wish without estate tax or gift tax. Charitable donations don't appear on the government's tax radar either, whether they be bequeathed in estates or presented as outright gifts.

Because the gift tax is tied to the estate tax, you can make gifts during your lifetime, but you must keep track of them. They count against the eventual estate tax exemption amount. If you set up a trust for the kids with $5 million a few years ago, because of the inflation adjustment, you can, in 2017, make a new gift to add enough to the trust to bring it up to the $5.49 million exemption amount. You can do the same thing in future years if the exemption amount continues to be adjusted for inflation.

Assuming they had not made any prior gifts in their lifetimes, a couple could gift $10.98 million tax-free in 2017 since husbands and wives each have separate exemptions. Did you know that you can make gifts for educational expenses or medical costs in an unlimited amount? The only caveat is that you must pay the facility or entity that rendered the care directly. Paying a family member directly won't work. If you don't do it right, you will forfeit the exclusion, and you may have to file a tax return.

The Unified Tax Credit

The unified tax credit is so named because it combines the federal gift tax and the estate tax into one unified tax arrangement. If, for example, you give in excess of the annual gift tax exclusion amount in any year, you can pay the tax on the excess or avoid paying the tax by taking advantage of the unified credit. The unified credit enables you to give away $5.49

million (as of 2017) during your lifetime, tax-free. Of course, when you use the unified tax credit during your lifetime, you reduce the amount by which you may offset estate taxes your heirs will incur when you die.

Life Insurance Strategies

A strategy that is becoming more and more popular these days is to include life insurance as part of an overall wealth protection plan. One reason for this is that life insurance comes with tax advantages other financial instruments do not possess. An individual can take today's wealth and, using life insurance, leverage it to cover the estate taxes of a large estate or create a large estate down the road.

Think about it this way. When does an estate plan take effect? When you die, of course. Life insurance policies pay off at the same time. It is a mistake to say that life insurance is altogether tax-free. It is income tax-free. The proceeds from a life insurance policy are subject to federal estate taxes, which are much higher (up to 50 percent) than the rates for income tax. Would you believe that the IRS collects more money from improperly titled life insurance proceeds than they do from any other source, including real estate and liquidated stocks and bonds? It's true.

What do we mean by "improperly titled" life insurance? Life insurance policies are owned, like any other asset. But you can own them in a way that keeps them out of your taxable estate, or you can own them in such a way as to make their payouts subject to the estate tax.

The Irrevocable Life Insurance Trust

Why not let a trust own the life insurance policy and also be the policy's beneficiary? That way it's out of your taxable estate. It cannot be just any trust. It must be an irrevocable life insurance trust (ILIT). This has to be properly structured, but it can ensure the proceeds of the life insurance policy are used to do a number of things, including provide an income stream; pay off mortgages, debts, and ordinary estate taxes; and keep the assets available for use by the family.

From an estate planning perspective, an ILIT can use insurance proceeds to convert illiquid assets, such as real estate, or shares of a family business into liquid assets. This kind of liquidation (purchase) is viewed as a tax-neutral exchange since no taxes will be due on the asset itself.

The ILIT can lend money to your estate, a loan that is secured by the estate's assets. The loan can be used to pay estate taxes due on other assets. An insurance trust will make it so creditors of the surviving spouse or any other estate raiders, including greedy relatives, will have no access to the funds. This fends off possible lawsuits, potential divorces, and even bankruptcies. The ILIT acts as a shield for the estate for many generations. The death benefit of the ILIT is also typically structured to cover your estate tax liability, keeping your heirs from having to sell your assets, often at a reduced rate, to pay the estate taxes.

If you want the trust to be structured with the long term in view, purchasing a life insurance policy makes the most sense. In addition to the leveraging the premium dollar paid in, the life insurance also generates no taxable income to the trust. If you were to put mutual funds or other investment accounts into an irrevocable trust, they would generate dividends or capital gains, which are taxed at the highest rate possible since it is in the trust.

ILIT Requirements
Certain requirements come with ILITs, and you need to know what they are and make sure your documents adhere to them if you want your insurance trust to effectively protect your assets.

Funding the ILIT
An unfunded trust is like an empty shell. You have to fund the ILIT with the life insurance policy. How? If you personally own the life insurance contract in question, you must contact the carrier and have them title the policy to the trust. You must also make the trust the beneficiary. Wait a minute! Didn't I just unprotect my spouse or my children? No. Now you will make your spouse, your children, or the other individual in whom you have an insurable interest as the beneficiary or beneficiaries of the trust. They will eventually receive the proceeds of the insurance policy benefits as directed by the provisions of the trust.

If you were the prior owner of the policy before transferring ownership to the trust, you must now allow the ILIT to pay the premiums. This establishes ownership in the eyes of the court and prevents creditors or other claimants from raiding your assets. You may have to make an annual gift to the trust, which in turn allows the trust to make the premium payments. A competent financial advisor will know how to minimize or perhaps eliminate any gift tax that you may owe as a consequence of this annual gift.

A word of caution in setting up ownership of the ILIT: if it is your life that is insured, you cannot also be a trustee of the ILIT. You have to name your spouse, one of your adult children, or some other trusted individual as trustee. You want to make sure that whomever you select for this job will follow the instructions of the trust and pay the premiums on time. If you're using your spouse as trustee, make sure to consult with your attorney as to how to fund the trust carefully to avoid the trust from being included in your estate value.

There are many flavors of irrevocable trust planning that can come into play. Aside from an ILIT, a spousal limited access trust (SLAT) is also a common variation. Essentially, each spouse creates a separate trust, and funds it with individually owned assets. In this structure, after one spouse passes away, there are provisions in the trust that allow the surviving spouse to take income from the trust as needed. The assets remain held outside of the estate, but some families appreciate the additional flexibility this provides.

Creating an Income Stream

Is there a way to use an ILIT to provide an income stream while you are alive? Yes, if it is structured correctly. As stated above, you cannot be the trustee of the ILIT. According to the wording of the trust, only its beneficiaries are eligible to access the cash values of the life insurance policy during the life of the insured. So, if the policy insures your life, you cannot personally access its cash values. But your spouse could access the cash values if she is listed as a beneficiary. Sometimes the insurance policy insures two lives, as in a survivorship or second-to-die policies. In these cases, the children or grandchildren can have access to the policy's cash values if they are also its beneficiaries.

Dr. and Dr. Anderson: A Case Study

Take the case of one couple who both happen to be physicians. The Andersons are age seventy-one and seventy and have an estate valued at approximately $13 million. Both are retired and living comfortably on a combined income of $150,000 from pensions and Social Security. Their objectives are to minimize estate taxes and maximize their legacy to their children. The Andersons have two adult children, also physicians, and four grandchildren.

The Anderson's $13 million estate have unified tax credits of $10.98 million ($5.49 million each), which leaves $2 million that would be taxable. Federal estate taxes of 40 percent would cost their estate $800,000. Their combined Illinois estate tax exemption is $8 million ($4 million each), meaning there would be roughly another $592,000 due in Illinois estate taxes for a combined tax liability of roughly $1.39 million, not including probate and settlement costs.

Maximizing the Estate

The Andersons implemented what we call a lifetime exemption trust to maximize their estate. For this to work, the trust had to be irrevocable. Through the trust, which is outside the estate, the Andersons gifted $2 million tax-free into the trust and purchased a $10.6 million life insurance policy. By doing this, they reduced their lifetime exemption by about $2 million (not factoring in the $14,000 annual exclusions) and reduced their estate by that same amount. Through the purchase of life insurance, they were able to provide a guaranteed death benefit, which could be used to pay the estate taxes and leverage the money in the most tax-advantaged way possible.

What effect would this have on the Anderson's estate? By implementing this simple strategy, the Andersons are able to leverage their estate for their heirs from about $11.5 million to $20 million, after tax. The life insurance was now held outside of the estate, ensuring the death benefit would be paid income- and estate tax-free to their heirs.

Drs. Anderson also have asset protection concerns, not just for themselves but also for their heirs. Even though they have good malpractice insurance, they felt it necessary to protect themselves as much as possible from potential lawsuits. The trust strategy facilitated this and ensures this money will be protected from would-be creditors against them and their children.

Heirs Receive: $11.53 million vs. **$20.13 million**

Case Study: Mr. and Dr. Smith

This case also has to do with estate maximization and avoiding the estate tax as well as how to best deal with your qualified retirement accounts and the income tax liability within them. It could also be called the "80 percent IRA tax trap."

Dr. Smith and her husband are ages sixty-five and sixty-seven, respectively. They have $2 million in IRAs. They live comfortably on a combined income of $120,000 and have no need for their RMDs that they will have to take beginning at age seventy and a half. They have three adult children and six grandchildren.

Their objectives are to maximize their IRAs for the benefit of their heirs, avoid taxes, and protect the assets of their estate from such things as divorce, lawsuits, or liability. From a legacy standpoint, their IRAs were subject to as much as 40 percent income tax and 40 percent estate tax. That meant that, without any further planning, their heirs stood to receive only $488,000 out of their $2 million investment, not including state estate taxes, if they were to pass away. Another problem lay in the fact that their money was at risk. For every dollar the Smiths risk, they are in jeopardy of losing that dollar. The IRAs were tax-deferred, which meant that transferring them to heirs would cause a taxable event. The best-case scenario for the Smiths would be for their heirs to receive 24 percent of the IRA after taxes if they took the money as a lump sum, and the worst case would be for the heirs to receive nothing if it were all lost in the stock market.

The solution was to go ahead and liquidate the IRAs, pay the 40 percent income tax, and use the net remaining $1.2 million to establish a children's trust. By using the tax-free power of life insurance benefits, the children were now in position to receive a $7.2 million death benefit upon their parents' death, income- and estate tax-free.

In this scenario, the clients wanted to liquidate the entire IRA and were comfortable with paying the large income tax at one time. Another option to spread out and minimize the income tax burden would have been to take annual distributions from the IRA to fund the children's trust. The distributions could be planned to maintain a certain income tax rate or just to spread out the distributions over, say five, seven, or ten years.

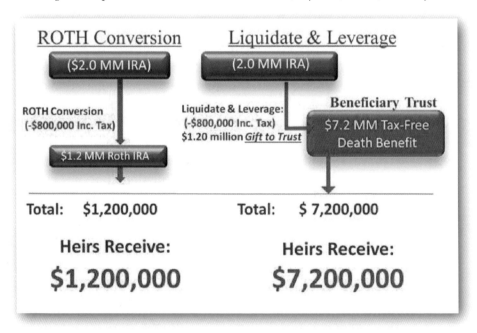

CHAPTER 14

MAXIMIZE THE BENEFIT OF CHARITABLE GIVING

C haritable giving has always been a means by which Americans show their passion for causes they cherish. This type of generosity is commendable and says something about the American spirit. The problem is that some don't know the best ways to give, both for the charity, and to maximize the personal benefit. Part of estate planning is to make these gifts so that we not only are able to provide the most benefit to the organizations we are passionate about but also to reap the tax benefits granted by the IRS for such giving, both for ourselves and our heirs.

Uncle Sam encourages such giving by offering us tax deductions when we give to a charity that qualifies under section 501(c)(3) as a charitable organization. The IRS tax code goes further to distinguish between private charities, such as family foundations, and public charities, like hospitals, churches, and universities. For example, when you donate to a university or hospital, you can deduct the entire amount from your AGI. If you give more than your annual AGI, you may apply the excess to future income for five years.

There are tremendous tax benefits for gifts left to a charity through a trust or an annuity. These are called "indirect gifts." There is nothing secret about this information. It is all right there in the tax code. But you would be amazed at how many people I run across who have no idea that such provisions exist. By giving through irrevocable charitable remainder trusts (CRTs) or annuities, it is possible to maximize the benefits of your philanthropy for not only the organization to which you are giving but also for your heirs.

Charitable Remainder Trusts

While there are many ways to give to charities, a CRT is one of the best from an estate planning point of view because few strategies enable the giver to maximize the personal, financial, and tax benefits as well.

With a CRT, it may be possible to receive a deduction for your gift to your favorite charity while at the same time creating a lifetime stream of income. You can also avoid paying capital gains taxes on the sale or disposition of appreciated securities or other property with effective CRT planning. In addition, a CRT can play an important role in your estate by reducing your potential estate tax liability.

The way a CRT works is pretty simple. Once a qualified attorney writes the trust, highly appreciated assets are moved into the trust, avoiding capital gains and providing you, the donor, with an income tax deduction that can be spread out over five years. You are able to name a beneficiary to receive a yearly income stream from the trust, and upon your death, the remainder of the CRT will go to the specified charities. Since the assets were transferred out of your estate, the charitable trust may also reduce your estate tax liability. However, one drawback of a CRT is that it isn't designed to leave any of the remainder interest to children. This can be remedied by electing to take distributions from the trust and using them to fund a separate life insurance policy for the benefit of your children.

Let's look at an example of how this works. Dr. and Mrs. Jones are sixty-five and sixty years old, respectively, with an estate valued at $13 million. Their estate includes $3 million in highly appreciated assets. They are living comfortably from the proceeds of a pension, IRAs, and rental income, but they would like to maximize the value of the appreciated assets as a legacy to their children and their favorite charities. The illustration below shows how a CRT strategy helps them meet these objectives.

By setting up a CRT and gifting $3 million to the trust, the Joneses were able to have an income tax deduction of up to a 50 percent of their

AGI spread over five years. The gift to the CRT will also reduce the size of their estate to below the unified credit, eliminating federal estate tax liability.

Next, by electing to take a 5 percent payout ($150,000 per year) from the CRT and gifting it to a separate children's trust, they can purchase a $9 million life insurance policy for the benefit of their children. At their death, Dr. and Mrs. Jones will have $0 estate tax liability, and they will have provided their favorite charities with a $3 million gift (assuming the assets in the trust earn 5 percent). Their children will receive a $9 million tax-free gift in addition to their $10 million estate.

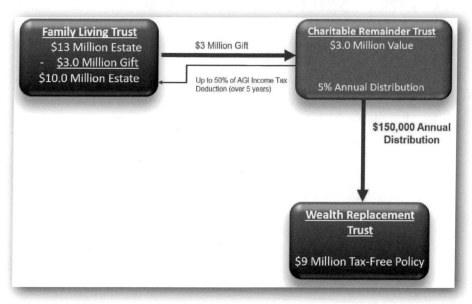

CHAPTER 15

TOOLS FOR PROTECTING YOUR ASSETS

What is the point of working hard all your life to establish wealth if you cannot protect it? Many today are forming family limited partnerships (FLPs) and limited liability companies (LLCs) in order to control and protect their assets from lawsuits and creditors. These measures can also reduce tax liabilities when it comes to gifts and the estate tax. I know of few legal strategies that offer the advantages of wealth protection as an LLC.

A family LLC gives its owners protection from creditors and can often save a considerable amount in the way of estate and gift taxes. Family LLCs usually have multiple owners, all of whom are related to each other (thus the name). Family LLCs can do many things, but one of the most useful is to facilitate the transfer property from one or more individuals to the LLC. For example, older family members can transfer assets that are titled in their names to the LLC. This type of capitalization of the LLC is generally a tax-free event and helps older family members gradually transfer partial ownership of assets to children. This makes it easier for family members to manage assets and avoid unnecessary taxes. Assets also held in a family LLC are protected from creditors. Estate raiders cannot get at the assets of an LLC the same way they could those owned by a person or persons.

Divorce can cause sticky situations among family members. LLC members can use a buy/sell agreement among them to prevent the untimely sale or transfer of membership interests resulting from the divorce of a child. Operating agreements can be amended as necessary, giving owners considerable operating flexibility when circumstances change. This is in sharp contrast to an irrevocable trust, the provisions of which are locked in place.

Some worry about giving children immediate access to transferred assets. They will be comforted to learn that the LLC's operating agreement can contain provisions to prevent members from easily cashing out their interests. The LLC can control distributions of the assets. The operating agreement of the LLC is restrictive in nature and serves as the point of control over the function of the LLC. For example, the operating agreement prohibits a member from withdrawing from or dissolving the company. It keeps creditors from initiating certain court proceedings against a member (judgments). Another advantage of the family LLC is that it simplifies the process of gifting to your children. It is much easier to gift an interest in the LLC than it is to gift individual assets.

Is an active business necessary in order to form an LLC? Not necessarily. Anyone can transfer personal assets to an LLC and have the same benefits as the business owner. What can a family LLC own? Nearly anything! But the most common assets a family LLC will hold are usually such things as investments, real estate, and brokerage accounts.

How Family LLCs Function

Family LLC owners are called "members" in the charter and bylaws. Each member is entitled to his or her share of distributions, but instructions contained in the document govern control of the LLC's actual operation. This allows the original owner to maintain control over the assets of the LLC by a separate management entity, if desired. In other words, a parent can maintain control of the entity even if the children own the majority of the membership interests. The initial member is usually the original owner's living trust. The original owner may sell or gift membership interests to the children or their trusts for their benefit.

When it comes to forming a family LLC or an FLP, depending on which you choose to use, you should consult a professional who has a considerable amount of training in this area. This type of LLC is much more complex than a single-member LLC, which a small business owner may establish for the purposes of insulating himself or herself from personal liability.

Avoiding Probate

Another reason why FLPs and LLCs are great estate planning tools has to do with the probate process. The courts are only concerned with your personal assets after your death. So it comes down to ownership. An LLC allows you to gift property without giving up control. It allows you to remove your assets from your estate and place them in an entity, but you must ensure that proper planning is done to maintain the annual gifting.

Valuation Discounting

The idea here is that what an asset is worth is subjective. Valuation discounting, as an estate planning tool, allows you to adjust the perceived value of an asset so you can gift more tax-free each year. If the current (as of 2015) ceiling on tax-free gifts to an individual is $14,000, an asset owned by a family LLC is discounted. For one thing, it is less marketable.

The more liquid and readily tradable an asset is, the more valuable it is. If an LLC or an FLP owns an asset, it lacks marketability because ownership of the asset is spread among those owning an interest in the LLC. That means it is deemed to be of less value because it cannot be easily traded, sold, or converted to cash because of the lack of interest in an asset with such encumbrances. A member of an LLC or partner in a FLP cannot easily transfer his or her interest in an asset owned by the entity because state law requires the approval of the other members or partners.

Another factor contributing to discounting the valuation of an asset held by an LLC or FLP is the lack of control of that asset. Just because you are a member of an entity doesn't mean you can liquidate an asset it owns. An LLC's manager(s), who may or may not be members, control it. The general partner(s) controls the FLP. They can be designed as manager in the operating agreement. The manager(s) control the entity independent of its partners (FLP) or members (LLC). That lack of control over an asset affects its value. This separation of control from ownership makes it possible to gift almost all of the value that would otherwise be included in a taxable estate without losing control of the underlying asset.

Imagine, for example, that an LLC owns a piece of real property worth $1,000. One member, whom we will call Bill and is not a manager, owns 10 percent interest in the LLC. If the LLC sells the property and liquidates it, Bill would receive $100 because that is the liquidation value of his interest. Here's where discounting comes in.

What if Bill wants to gift his 10 percent interest in the LLC to his son, Billy? Assuming the other members of the LLC are family members and willing to allow Billy to become a member, they may discount the value of the property substantially based on the reasons cited above. These discounts can be taken at the time a gift of partnership interest is made from one partner to another and upon the death of one partner on their remaining interests. Calculating the discount rate to be applied are determined by the specific language inside of the partnership agreement as well as the assets owned by the partnership. Typically, discount rates range between 30 and 40 percent, but could be much higher.

Jeff: A Case Study

Jeff was able to reduce the perceived value of his estate for tax purposes through the creation of a FLP. Jeff's estate was valued at around $7 million. This included an investment property worth approximately $2 million. Jeff's objective was to retain control of the investment property but develop a plan to remove it from his estate and transfer it to his son and daughter.

Jeff sought professional help in establishing an FLP and transferred the $2 million investment property into it. It was determined that the FLP would be created with two thousand shares, each valued at $1,000. Jeff would retain all management control but could begin to transfer ownership to his children a little at a time.

The valuation discounting would become a powerful part of Jeff's estate planning at this point. If we assume a 33 percent discount is taken on the value of the $1,000 units, then under tax laws current at the time, Jeff could gift up to $14,000 per year to each of his children, which would normally equal fourteen shares, or units, of the FLP. But once we factor in the valuation discounting of 33 percent, this discounting rate allows Jeff to more quickly transfer ownership of his estate and considerably reduce his estate tax liability.

CHAPTER 16

SOLVING FINANCIAL PROBLEMS ONE PUZZLE PIECE AT A TIME

O ne of the things I admire about Steve Jobs, the late brainchild of Apple, is that it was never about the money with him. When he was twenty-two years old, he had nothing. Three years later, he was worth over $100 million. He almost seemed uncomfortable with his fortune, however. What drove him was creating life-improving products that could make a difference. The money was a side effect. He is reported to have said at one point, "Being the richest man in the cemetery doesn't matter to me. Going to bed at night saying we've done something wonderful. That's what matters to me." [7]

Among the many lessons we can learn from looking at the body of work that Jobs left behind is that solutions to problems often require taking a fresh look at them and assembling the tools that are right in front of us. In the field of financial planning, that is certainly the case. I find so often that the problem is not so much a problem in the sense that it is a difficulty that needs to be overcome as it is a puzzle that needs to be solved by finding the right pieces. What we call the problem is finding a way to make the financial wishes of a client become a reality. The problem often presents scenarios that involve people, money, and time. Just as the competency of an architect can be measured by how well a building is designed and constructed, the competency of financial advisors

---

7 (https://en.wikiquote.org/wiki/Steve_Jobs)

can be measured by their ability to recognize the tools and products that have been right there all along and just need to be assembled in such a way as to achieve the desired result.

Many of the case examples you have seen in this book are based on true-life situations that people experience every day in their financial lives. Usually their wishes on how they want to dispose of their assets are no more complicated than a desire to be comfortable and independent during their sunset years and a want to pass as much as possible along to their loved ones when they die. There is nothing complex about that.

Where the complexity lies is wrangling with the rules and limitations put in place by the monetary system of which we are all a part. There are natural laws at work, those of supply and demand. The often-unpredictable ebb and flow of our markets are evidence of these natural laws. There are also estate and tax laws in place that are subject to frequent change, which require a thorough understanding of their complexities.

The job of your financial advisor is to know and understand the laws that are in place and the tools that are available to help solve the puzzle. Every investment and estate planning tool has its fair share of pros and cons, and it is critical for an advisor to have a thorough understanding of them to provide the client with the best options.

I don't pretend to know exactly how the minute cause-and-effect cogs and gears of our national economy work anymore than I recognize the answers to loftier astronomical questions, like why the sun is 93 million miles away from the earth or how the gravitational force of faraway planets affects our earth. I just know from studying physics and astronomy that those things are the case. If the art of financial planning is understanding and moving with the natural laws of economics, the science of it comes from understanding and maneuvering through the ones that are put in place by lawmakers and are continually subject to change.

My role when it comes to growing wealth for my clients and preserving and protecting that wealth once it has been acquired is a simple matter of learning and understanding the rules, natural and man-made, that affect that process and using them to my client's advantage. Like doctors taking the Hippocratic Oath, my first obligation—at least from my point of view—is to "do no harm." In other words, make sure you don't lose money. After that, it is to find a way to achieve as much growth as possible from those assets while at the same time making sure that you don't outlive them. The real-life situations you see in the pages of this book are just a few that have been compiled from case files where problems were solved by combining one or more financial concepts or retirement products the same way a chemist achieves a desired result by combining two or more elements to produce a new compound. Put any name you wish on the mechanism that is produced. The result is what's important.

Learning the secret of how to do some of the most important things in life is often a matter of knowing the people who know. The secret of how to successfully manage our financial affairs is actually no secret at all. Just as a very complex engine can be made to run more smoothly and proficiently with just a little tweaking here and there by a skilled mechanic who knows how and where to turn the right knobs and screws, a skilled financial planner can rescue a financial plan that is off track from its stated goals and, with just a few course adjustments and strategy or two, set it sailing properly again.

About the Author

Michael Jankowski, A frequent seminar leader and lecturer, Michael specializes in working with physicians, business owners, and corporate executives. He is the President and CEO of Wealth Planning Network, Chicagoland's premier wealth management and estate planning firm. Michael has been a financial advisor in the area for over 25 years, and has successfully helped hundreds of affluent families achieve their financial and estate planning goals. Through a combination of personalized attention, industry expertise, and the latest technology, Michael and his team, along with Chicagoland's premier attorneys and CPA's, provide a complete financial and estate plan that is tailored to meet the unique goals of each client. He specializes in asset protection, estate and income tax minimization, investment management, and charitable giving strategies to maximize his clients' assets throughout their lives and to their heirs. Michael is a native resident of the Chicagoland area, currently residing in Western Springs with his wife Chrisy and their many children.